# YORKSHIRE
# Terrier
## AN OWNER'S GUIDE

# The authors

**Robert Killick** is a prominent breeder and exhibitor of Welsh Terriers, winning at the major Championship shows. He has a Judges Diploma (Credit) and judges all breeds at Open Show level and his own breed at Championship level.

After a lifetime in the theatre as a stage manager, director and actor, he turned to freelance journalism. In 1990, he became a weekly columnist for the UK canine newspaper *Our Dogs*. He also writes monthly columns in *Dogworld USA*, the world's largest circulating dog magazine, and the Swedish magazine *Hundesport*, and is a feature writer for *Dogs Today* in the UK.

In 1994, his poems were published by the American National Library of Poetry for which he received the award of 'Poet of Merit' from the International Society of Poets, and he was nominated for 'Poet of the Year' in 1995.

**John Bower BVSc, MRCVS** is a senior partner in a small animal Veterinary Hospital in Plymouth, England. He has served as President of both the British Veterinary Association and the British Small Animal Veterinary Association. He writes regularly for the veterinary press and also for dog and cat publications. He is co-author of two dog healthcare books and a member of the Kennel Club.

**Caroline Bower BVM&S, MRCVS** runs a veterinary health centre in the same practice as John. Her special interests include prevention and treatment of behavioural problems, and she lectures to dog breeding and training groups.

 Collins

# YORKSHIRE
# Terrier

## AN OWNER'S GUIDE

Robert Killick

## DEDICATION

For my daughter, Alicja, who, like my dogs, is a continual joy.

## AUTHOR'S ACKNOWLEDGEMENTS

For many years Yorkshire Terrier breeders have consistently been kind and informative to me. My thanks to all of them in the preparation of this book. Special thanks to Osman Sameja, a gentle soul who placed his immense knowledge at my disposal wholeheartedly, and to Terry and Mary Cole whose in-depth knowledge of the birth of Yorkies was so freely given. Finally my gratitude to Clifford (Doggy) Hubbard who gave me access to his library, the biggest collection of dog books in the world.

First published in hardback in 1996 by
Collins, an imprint of
HarperCollins*Publishers*
77-85 Fulham Palace Road
Hammersmith, London W6 8JB
The Collins website address is www.collins.co.uk
Collins is a registered trademark of HarperCollins Publishers Limited
First published in paperback in 1998
This edition first published in 2003

09  08  07  06  05  04
9  8  7  6  5  4  3  2

A catalogue record of this book is available from the British Library.

ISBN 0 00 717606 6

This book was created by SP Creative Design for HarperCollins*Publishers* Ltd
Editor: Heather Thomas
Designers: Al Rockall and Rolando Ugolini
Production: Rolando Ugolini
Illustrations: Al Rockall and Rolando Ugolini

**Photography:**
David Dalton: back cover and pages 3, 11, 12, 16, 17, 20-21, 31, 33, 37, 42, 43, 44, 45, 50, 51, 52, 53, 54, 55, 60, 61, 63, 66, 69, 70, 71, 72, 73, 76, 78, 84
François Nicaise: front and back covers and pages 1, 6-7, 9, 10, 13, 14, 19, 23, 24, 27, 29, 30, 32, 35, 36, 38-39, 41, 46, 47, 48, 49, 57, 59, 65, 75, 82, 83, 87, 89, 90, 91, 92, 94-95

**Acknowledgements**
The publishers would like to thank the following for their kind assistance in producing this book: Scampers School for Dogs for their help with photography, and special thanks to Charlie Clarricoates for all his hard work. Elizabeth Quinn and her dog Joey, Mr & Mrs Raynes and their dog Sammy and Doreen Johnson and her Lyndoney Yorkshire Terriers for appearing in the special photography.

Colour reproduction by Colourscan, Singapore
Printed and bound by Printing Express Ltd, Hong Kong

# CONTENTS

# PART ONE

# YOU AND YOUR DOG

The Yorkshire Terrier is one of the world's best-loved dogs and a very popular family pet. Fun-loving and intelligent, the Yorkie has great spirit and character for such a tiny dog – he should not weigh more than 3.1 kg (7 lb) maximum. Yorkies are extremely loyal and make excellent companions with their playful and inquisitive nature. In spite of their size and glamorous appearance, they need regular exercise and stimulating games to occupy them. Like all terriers, they are game little dogs and enjoy hunting and disappearing underground down holes in pursuit of their prey!

1

# THE HISTORY OF THE BREED

## ORIGINS OF THE YORKSHIRE TERRIER

Looking at a Yorkshire Terrier, it is little short of miraculous that the tiny glamorous dog so fetchingly filling our lives could have had its beginnings in the dank, cold tunnels of mines and dark mills of the Northern industrial towns where its purpose was to kill the rats that bred in their thousands and plagued the workers, causing disease and illness in the mid-nineteenth century.

From the dog small enough to slip out of sight in a miner's pocket to today's elegant, silky-haired, pampered animal, which is one of the most important companion breeds in the world, is a story of the patience and skill of the working men of England. They had no idea that their little terrier dog would be so popular; in those days it didn't matter how it looked provided that it could do the job for which it was bred.

### Underground dogs

There are people today who don't like to think of their pretty little dog being associated with rough terriers but the fact cannot be avoided. Although the Yorkshire Terrier is formally in the Toy Group, its ancestors were common terriers. Small, fierce terrier-type dogs have frequented the British Isles since before recorded history; they were kept around the homesteads and workers' homes to keep down rats and other animals, such as foxes, which were a danger to poultry and lambs. How terriers came into being is an enigma which may never be explained; the word itself comes from the Latin word 'terra', meaning earth; hence dogs that will go underground in pursuit of their prey. Anyone who owns a terrier will know how difficult it is to prevent them from diving into holes in the ground even if they have never seen one before. Even the modern Yorkshire Terrier will not be averse to going underground when out walking, as the hunting instinct does

*The Yorkshire Terrier is a bright-eyed, mischievous companion and makes the perfect small pet.*

not diminish with the size of the dog.

There are many woodcuts and prints from mediaeval times depicting men hunting foxes and badgers with terriers to drive the animals from their lairs. In this enlightened age, baiting badgers is illegal and the hunting of foxes is a dying activity, but in order to understand the terrier, it is essential to know about its bloody past and what was expected of those early dogs. The behaviour and characteristics of your pet or showdog are inextricably linked with its function at the beginning of its development. The terrier's hunting ability was bred for by selection and only the best dogs were kept for work; so well were these

*The Yorkie has a spirited look and is always ready for anything, especially walks and games.*

characteristics fixed that the majority of terriers carry the instinct to a greater or lesser degree to this day.

It is of immense significance that the British Isles is the only place in the world that developed terriers. Every terrier breed derives from Britain and Ireland, although nobody has a clue how they were developed. For hundreds of years, local terriers of different types were bred all over these islands, resulting in the twenty-five breeds recognised throughout the world today.

## EARLY DAYS

The Phoenicians, based on the coast of Syria a thousand years before the birth of Christ, were the first great wandering traders. They sailed the known world, clinging to the Mediterranean and Atlantic coasts and sometimes dogs were kept on their ships. Some would have escaped at various ports or may have even been traded. Ships were occasionally lost at sea, and dogs might have scrambled ashore after shipwrecks, injecting new blood into the local dog population. It is known that the Phoenicians took a toy dog to Malta and from that evolved the white Maltese, which was originally known as the Maltese Terrier. Some of those early dogs who may have been a different colour could have found themselves in the British Isles, introduced by traders or returning Crusaders.

The rampaging Celts and other tribes that invaded Britain would have brought their own dogs. The Vikings colonized great sections of the country, and the Scottish islands, the Isle of Man and Dublin were Viking colonies peopled by the families of the invaders; they, too, brought dogs with them, as did world conquerors,

such as the Romans, who collected dogs from conquered countries. The Normans introduced their native dogs into Britain in such numbers that they had an influence on the indigenous breeds. The development of individual breeds usually took place over many years, sometimes hundreds, and was often the result of happy accidents. The resultant dogs were then used in their various fields of work and their proficiency recognised; astute breeders, recognising the traits, would develop them further and type was slowly fixed.

### The nineteenth century

That today's Yorkshire Terrier is a manufactured breed is not in dispute, but the difference between the development of the dog as we know it and gundogs, for instance, was that it all happened in a comparatively short time. The breed did not have an official name until 1870 when Angus Sutherland, writing in the magazine *The Field,* suggested after a famous big-winning dog, 'Mozart', won a variety class at the Westmorland Show that because so many of the best dogs came from Yorkshire they should be called 'Yorkshire Terriers'. The name stuck and it wasn't long before it came into general usage among dog owners.

Early canine writers from the turn of the century looked into the breed's antecedents; obviously they were closer to the original breeders than we are today, but despite all their efforts they were unable to find hard evidence of which breeds made up the ingredients of the Yorkie, as it is affectionately known. Much of their writings were based on kennel gossip and rumour but would have contained a grain of truth. The main development came from the working people at the time of the industrial revolution. We know that education for the working classes at that time was virtually non-existent and few people, if anyone, kept records of their breeding experiments; such information would have been kept secret. Even today, some breeders will not divulge all their knowledge because they don't want their competitors to get an edge on them.

Once a breeder consistently produced the sought-after attributes, the fewer people who knew how it was achieved, the bigger the price they commanded. It is on record that second-class specimens of Yorkshire Terriers would fetch up to thirty guineas, which was a large amount of money in the late-nineteenth century. Inferior dogs were sold

because breeders had the sense to keep the best in order to reproduce quality. Extra money for a poor family from the sale of puppies would have been welcome.

*He may only be small but this Yorkshire Terrier has been romping through the countryside and enjoying a swim in a pond and a roll in the mud!*

## Clues to origins

The use of the word 'terrier' in its name is sufficient evidence that the early writers knew that terriers were used in the Yorkie's make-up. From contemporary published articles, we can pick up clues and form an opinion which is probably close to the truth. As far back as ancient Greek times, there were known terrier-type dogs with long, soft coats, and their genes are in the make-up of today's dogs. Small silky, long-haired terriers were the delight of the ladies of the court of King Henry VIII, and their coat was mentioned in the first published book of dogs, *Of Englishe Dogges* by King Henry's court physician, Johannes Caius.

The Yorkshire people have long had the reputation of being superb stockmen with a seemingly innate knowledge of how to breed fine animals. Couple this with their crafty business sense and it is possible to see how they recognised the possibilities of a small working dog. Poachers who risked deportation wanted very small terriers that could go down into rabbit holes, bolt the inhabitants into a net and then be hidden inside a jacket. However, the dog was still not yet the exquisite little gem so prized today.

*This Yorkshire Terrier is an old-fashioned working type, with a longer back than that of most of today's show dogs.*

## SCOTTISH TERRIERS

Some authorities believe that the Highland Terrier of Scotland had some input into the breed; without doubt, there were links. The great centres of the industrial revolution were in the North, the Midlands and South Wales and it was to these areas that the starving agricultural labourers and poorly paid Scottish workers gravitated, looking for a better standard of living. Workers in the cotton industry and miners from the River Clyde area of Scotland travelled to Leeds and Bradford searching for work, and they took their native terriers with them, particularly the Clydesdale or Paisley Terrier, which is now extinct. This breed was lumped together with several others known as Skye Terriers, a far cry from the Skye Terrier of today. It has to be understood that the division between breeds was less critical or distinct at that time and dogs tended to be named after the area in which they were most common, The Clydesdale had a long, silky coat of steel grey with a golden tan head, feet and legs but was bigger and longer in the body than the modern Yorkshire Terrier. The scene was set for the start of a new and separate breed.

It took many years before the realisation dawned that lurking in the rough terrier was a dog that was capable of fulfilling the burgeoning need for extremely beautiful small pet dogs for the newly emerging middle classes.

## Antecedents

The ubiquitous terrier of the time was the extinct black and tan Broken-haired Terrier, sometimes known as the Old English Broken-haired Terrier, a rough dog whose name implies a wiry mixture of a coat. He was almost certainly the predecessor of the Welsh Terrier and the Airedale. Experts believe that we must look at this breed in order to uncover an important part of the Yorkshire Terrier's forebears. There was another very game farm dog of the early nineteenth century known as the Waterside Terrier, which may have been a branch of the Old English Broken-haired and probably made some contribution to the Yorkie. It was small, no more than about 2.7kg (6 lb) in weight, with a longish grizzled coat and silvery-coloured hair on the head. The great ratting black and tan terrier, known as the Manchester Terrier, was also in the first stages of refinement and could certainly have added his quota of genes to the ingredients.

'Stonehenge', which was the pen name of a canine writer of the mid-nineteenth century, wrote of this new breed, 'Sometimes (sic) his coat is of a silky texture and in this case the colours are blue-fawn or blue-tan'. The phrasing of this statement shows clearly that type was very mixed and that the long-coated, correctly coloured dogs did not always occur. Later, in a book published in 1872 entitled *Dogs of the British Isles*, Yorkshire Terriers were described in such detail that, apart from the cropped ears and weight, they were almost the exact replica of today's dogs.

It should be noted that the cropping of ears is now illegal and has been since the beginning of this century; severe penalties will be incurred by anyone indulging in this cruelty, and Yorkshire Terriers are bred with naturally erect ears.

Weights varied between 4.5 and 8.1 kg (10-18 lb). With animals of such various sizes at the early shows, some weighing twice as much as others, it is small wonder that they were not sure of the breed. This size difference caused consternation in the United States when the breed first made its appearance in the 1880s. By the turn of the century, the Yorkshire breeders had succeeded

*A hardy, game little dog, this Yorkshire Terrier is enjoying the wintry weather.*

in reducing the breed's size considerably and such was their skill that they were able to breed truer to type.

## Breed clubs

The first Yorkshire Terrier breed club was formed in 1898 with the purpose of producing a Breed Standard to ensure uniformity; show-winning dogs and their progeny were recorded in a Stud Book. It was then theoretically possible to trace the lines. The new club was a starting point but many of the sires and dams that produced progeny before the club was created had no known forebears, so information before that period was sketchy. This situation was not helped by the fact that the breed was shown in several different breed classes: Skye Terriers, Scotch Terriers and Toy Terriers.

### HUDDERSFIELD BEN

The one line that is possible to trace the furthest goes back to 1850 with a long-coated blue Clydesdale dog named Old Crab and a drop-eared Skye-type bitch named Old Kitty. They produced the most famous dog in the history of the breed, Huddersfield Ben, born in 1865. He was owned by Mrs M.A. Foster of Bradford, who was a breed expert, and set the pattern of future Yorkshire Terriers. Historians have since described him as the 'father of the breed'. Every so often a dog emerges in all breeds who stamps his quality on every puppy he sires, and Ben was one of these. He was used a great deal at stud and a study of his pedigree will give some indication of the intensity of in-breeding needed to fix type. Ben was not the only powerful influence. He didn't sire the very small dogs which eventually became so fashionable; other clever breeders were working in parallel lines.

## The smallest dogs

There were tiny dogs being shown before Huddersfield Ben (see above) was born, and Mrs Foster had the smallest dog on record at the time. This was 'Bradford Marie', who weighed in at 0.8 kg (1 lb 14 oz). She later bred an even smaller one of 0.68 kg (1 lb 8 oz) who was named 'Bradford Queen of the Toys'.

# THE BREED STANDARD

The Standard is a detailed description of an ideal dog, which is compiled by the Kennel Club. It should not be considered a blueprint because, as a living creature, no dog can replicate another; it is a guide to perfection. We know that perfection does not exist which is why we strive to breed better dogs as close to the Standard as possible.

The wording is often vague, and this is to the breed's advantage because it allows flexibility. Those who seek to buy puppies for exhibition or to breed them should immerse themselves in the breed and make a study of the Standard to familiarize themselves with its every nuance. A real insight into a breed is not gained overnight nor does it matter how much theoretical knowledge is acquired; this is one activity that demands 'hands on' experience. The thinking person will physically handle as many dogs as possible, will examine them, will groom them, and slowly will acquire an in-depth knowledge. If that same person brings puppies into the world, rears them, studies their development into adulthood, lives close to them and then, at the end, buries them after a full life, he will be the person who knows.

■ **Type** This is a word that is frequently used in relation to breeds of dogs and is another concept that some people find difficult to understand, but it should be considered in connection with the Standard. Everyone knows the meaning of the ordinary word 'type' when used in normal conversation, but related to dogs the word has an entirely different meaning. The expression 'lacking in breed type' means that a dog lacks some of the qualities that make up that breed. In this context, 'type' means the hundreds of points that, when put together, makes one breed distinguishable from all others. It is the opinion of leading authorities that 'type' is contained within the Standard.

It is the breeder/exhibitor who seeks perfection. The exhibitor hopes to buy perfection, whereas the pet owners, whose numbers far exceed the former, love their dog as he is, but many would like to know if their little pet could win a prize at Crufts. By reading about the ideal Yorkshire Terrier, many pet owners may want to try their hand at showing their dogs and then, who knows, may want to breed the perfect dog.

*This beautifully groomed and presented show dog has an indefinable air of superiority. Owners of show dogs try to aspire to the Standard.*

# THE BREED STANDARD

Published by courtesy of the Kennel Club

**General Appearance** Long-coated, coat hanging quite straight and evenly down each side, a parting extending from nose to end of tail. Very compact and neat, carriage very upright conveying an important air. General outline conveying impression of vigorous and well proportioned body.

**Characteristics** Alert, intelligent toy terrier.

**Temperament** Spirited with even disposition.

**Size** Weight up to 3.1 kgs (7 lbs).

**Colour** Dark steel blue (not silver blue), extending from occiput to root of tail, never mingled with fawn, bronze or dark hairs. Hair on chest rich, bright tan. All tan hair darker at the roots than in middle, shading to still lighter at tips.

**Tail** Customarily docked to medium length with plenty of hair, darker blue in colour than rest of body, especially at the end of tail. Carried a little higher than level of back.

**Hindquarters** Legs quite straight when viewed from behind, moderate turn of stifle. Well covered with hair of rich golden tan a few shades lighter at ends than at roots, not extending higher on hindlegs than stifles.

**Gait/Movement** Free with drive; straight action front and behind, retaining level topline.

**Feet** Round; nails black.

**Note:** Male animals should have two apparently normal testicles fully descended into the scrotum.

**Coat** Hair on body moderately long, perfectly straight (not wavy), glossy; fine silky texture, not woolly. Fall on head long, rich golden tan, deeper colour at sides of head, about ear roots and on muzzle where it should be very long. Tan on head not to extend on to neck, nor must any sooty or dark hair intermingle with any of tan.

**Body** Compact with moderate spring of rib, good loin. Level back.

**Head and Skull** Rather small and flat, not too prominent or round in skull, nor too long in muzzle; black nose.

**Ears** Small, V-shaped, carried erect, not too far apart, covered with short hair, colour very deep, rich tan.

**Eyes** Medium, dark, sparkling, with sharp intelligent expression and placed to look directly forward. Not prominent. Edge of eyelids dark.

**Mouth** Perfect, regular and complete scissor bite, i.e., upper teeth closely overlapping lower teeth and set square to the jaws. Teeth well placed with even jaws.

**Neck** Good reach.

**Forequarters** Well laid shoulders, legs straight, well covered with hair of rich golden tan a few shades lighter at ends than at roots, not extending higher on forelegs than elbow.

## FAULTS

Any departure from the foregoing points should be considered a fault and the seriousness with which the fault should be regarded should be in exact proportion to its degree.

21

# AN EXTENDED STANDARD

The Standard appears to be extremely comprehensive and, in fact, some close examination reveals the use of words varying in meaning which allows really vast differences in interpretation. It will mean different things to different people and is the reason that differing styles of dogs win in competition. What is certain is that the Standard does not call for exaggeration; moderation is the requirement. The original function must be considered, and both balance and symmetry are a prime necessity.

The expression 'very compact and neat' refers to the body. It is not intended to mean small although the breed must be small. It is a big dog contained in a small, powerful well-proportioned body. Neat refers to the conformation of the body and not a neat coat. The carriage should not just be upright but very upright and it should convey an air of self-importance. All terriers should be aware of everything going on around them; this is the alert and intelligent look. The word 'spirited' gives the game away – it should be on the edge of action without stepping over.

■ **Head** The shape of the head will directly control the position of the eyes and the ears. Because of the hairy presentation of the show dog it is not easy to assess the head. The shape of the skull is of paramount importance; a flattish skull is called for – a domed head or an apple head will cause the ears and the eyes to be wrongly placed. The stop is an important feature in determining expression; it is the point where the front of the head drops to meet the top of the muzzle between the eyes. It should be a slope but never a vertical or near-vertical step as in a Pointer, but nor should it be shallow like that of a Collie. A fairly substantial black nose is the requirement. Yorkies use their fine scenting abilities more than is generally thought.

■ **Eyes** The word 'medium' applies to the size in relation to the head, and they must be dark and almond shaped. The pigmentation of the eyelids, although mentioned as dark, should be near black. This is important for the expression. Sparkling eyes are full of curiosity.

■ **Ears** These are an important aspect of expression. Small ears are asked for – a relative term. They should be small but in proportion to the head which they adorn, not too close together and not spread apart as on a domed head. They should be pricked up as if the dog is ready for action.

■ **Mouth** The dog must have a strong jaw to do his job; over long and it

becomes snipy and weak, too short and
the teeth get cramped.

■ **Teeth** are vital for all dogs: they not
only allow the animal to catch, kill and
eat their prey but they are the sole
means of defence. Therefore they must
be properly placed and of the correct
size. Possibly the dog will never again be
used for its original function but that is

*This Yorkshire Terrier, with a full show
coat, shows alertness and intelligence
when exhibited in the show ring.*

no excuse for allowing a deterioration of
the mouth.

The British are not too fussed over one
or two missing pre-molars (those at the side
of the mouth) but in Europe they do not

like it and splendid dogs can be disqualified in some countries. This is a bit severe considering that ancient skulls showing missing teeth have been dug up and there is evidence of wolves with missing teeth, perhaps an evolutionary process.

■ **Neck** A good length neck which is in proportion to the body is an essential.

*Yorkies may be among the smallest dogs but they are naturally adventurous and full of curiosity.*

If the dog has well laid shoulder blades the neck should fit smoothly into the shoulders. Close study will reveal the angle of the neck to the body and the head on the top of the spine will, if correct, give a cocky (self-important) look. Very careful training is necessary to get the dog to appear like that in the ring. The importance of the setting of the head on the neck cannot be stressed too much from an aesthetic point of view.

■ **Body** The skeleton is a chassis from which the moving parts hang and to which the muscles operating those moving parts are attached. It must therefore be correctly formed and strong enough to bear the stresses. The backbone is the key: the ribs should spring out from their connection to the backbone and flatten at the sides; the chest should be deep reaching at least to the elbow. The word 'compact' alludes to the loin, the joining bit between the last rib and the thigh. This should be fairly short giving great strength – short rib cages are totally wrong.

■ **Gait/Movement, front and hindquarters** These sections have been put together because they are so inter-dependent, and failure in these parts will reflect on the efficiency of the others. With the right vertebrae for the breed, giving a retained top line on the move, correctly-angled joints, correct positioning of the forehand and the pelvis, the dog should produce the correct free movement with drive from the back legs. Straight action refers to straight leg joints, front and back; when moving towards or away from the observer, elbows should not protrude.

## COAT AND COLOUR

The coat is of ultimate importance, and when the Standard was first written a system of points was devised. Each section of the dog was awarded a certain number of points totalling one hundred. The system fell into disuse because it was possible to award both good and bad specimens an equal number of points. It is important to understand how much weight the fathers of the breed placed on the coat, its colour and texture. Half the total of points could be awarded in this area.

POINTS SYSTEM

| | |
|---|---|
| Formation and terrier appearance | 15 |
| Head | 10 |
| Colour of hair on body | 15 |
| Mouth | 5 |
| Richness of tan on head and legs | 15 |
| Legs and feet | 5 |
| Quantity and length of coat | 10 |
| Ears | 5 |
| Quality of texture of coat | 10 |
| Eyes | 5 |
| Tail (carriage of) | 5 |
| **Total of points** | **100** |

# THE SHOW DOG

Although the breed club was founded in 1898, it would be several years before shows offered classes devoted to the Yorkshire Terrier by name. They were still exhibited in mixed breed classes but they began to be appreciated as a separate breed as type became fixed and excellent specimens began to win. Slowly big names in both dogs and breeders began to emerge. One of the first great showdogs was a bitch, Sprig of Blossom, born in 1908 who won twenty-six Challenge Certificates. The famous old dog Huddersfield Ben was in the pedigree of many eminent Yorkshire terriers, including Champion Boy Blue whose coat measured 108 cm (36 in), measured from tip to tip across the shoulders. He sired Champion Mendham Peggy, the winner of twenty-five certificates.

Mrs Annie Swan of the Invincia kennels had an enormous influence on the breed reaching right into modern times, as did Lady Edith Windham (later Windham-Dawson) who bred some spectacular dogs and did a great deal to popularize the Yorkshire Terrier in the United States. In the post-war years, many influential kennels emerged because of the explosion in popularity of the breed, including Nell and Jack Latliff's Ravelin kennels, Joyce Mann's Craigsbank dogs from Scotland and Mary and John Hayes with their Chantmarles Yorkies in South Wales. The Blairsville kennel, owned by Brian and Rita Lister, had their first champion in 1967, culminating in their wonderful Champion Blairsville Royal Seal who won fifty Challenge Certificates and took the Toy Group and reserve Supreme Champion at Crufts in 1978.

Undoubtedly the most prestigious kennel of modern times is owned by Osman Sameja from London. He made his first Ozmilion champion in 1972 and in the succeeding years has created a total of thirty champions. On the way, he has smashed all records. He holds the record for dog Challenge Certificates – fifty-two with Ch Ozmilion Dedication who was top dog of 1987 and top-winning Yorkie of all time. Ch Verolian Temptress with Ozmilion, owned by his sister-in-law, Mrs Sameja-Hilliard, holds the bitch record of thirty-nine Challenge Certificates. Furthermore, Osman Sameja's line can be traced back to the great Huddersfield Ben who started it all.

*This perfectly turned-out show dog is waiting for the judge's examination. Many owners and their dogs have discovered the joys of showing.*

# CHAPTER TWO

# THE ORIGINS OF DOGS

## EVOLUTION OF THE DOG

Myth or fact, where do they meet? The evolution of dogs is a subject that has taxed the brains of canine palaeontologists, and it would be easy to think that, as dogs have been linked inextricably to humans since early man, there would be a great deal known. Not so; it could be said that the close relationship between dog and man has developed over 20,000 years but concrete knowledge begins only in the last 1,000 years and detailed breed knowledge since the eighteenth century. Evidence of the evolution of dogs is sparse, but equally sparse is evidence of how two disparate species, humans and dogs, should come to be so dependent on each other. Flesh, tissue and hair rarely survive the millions of years and up to now bones have revealed very little about how the canine evolved from the tree-dwelling animal that some experts believe to have been the forerunner of today's dogs.

### Sixty million years ago

Prehistoric creatures have to be examined against a fantastically hostile environment with few clues, and such evidence as exists is argued over by the scientists. However, there is no doubt that there were creatures known as *Credonta*, which means 'Flesh/Teeth', and there may have been as many as 300 different species which changed over the next twenty million years, some of which were able to modify themselves to suit ever-changing conditions but many of which became extinct. A strange looking animal, not unlike a polecat, known as Miacis took shape and is credited as being an ancestor of the dog. From this creature came Cynodictus and eventually the prototype dog, the Tomarctus. By the time the Eocene Period arrived, some animals were beginning to stabilize and could be recognisable today. They ranged in size and shape from great bear-like mammals to much smaller animals that resembled minks, some of which were tree dwellers.

Thirty million years would pass, and giant wolf-like creatures were to be found

*Yorkie puppies are especially appealing but you should never buy one on impulse because it looks cute.*

all over the world, but these disappeared to be replaced with smaller canids. Evolution continued inexorably and around seven million years ago the really significant divisions began. It is thought that the land-dwelling animals slowly split into two great groups: the first containing dogs, raccoons, bears, weasels and otters; whereas in the second group were cats, civets, genets and hyenas. Improbably, it seems there is a very remote relationship between dogs and cats.

## Man and the wolf/dog

The next part of the story needs real imagination. How did a wolf/dog type of animal get friendly with man? Imagine that it is dusk, and outside a cave a prehistoric family crouches round a fire, tearing at juicy steaks. They throw the discarded bones over their shoulders, and glittering eyes in the bushes mark the fall of each bone. Later, the family goes into the cave for the night and lurking wolf-like figures creep out and snatch up the bones. Contact has been made.

The wolf with its superior intelligence soon learnt that man was a good source of food and packs of wolves would follow hunting parties as scavengers. Man, a creature of greater intelligence than other animals, would recognise the wolf's

*Looking at the affectionate and friendly Yorkie, it is hard to believe that his ancestor was the wolf.*

hunting skills, its speed and its alertness around the dwelling. Modern thought is that dogs are descended from wolves although it is conceded that there are several quite different types of wolf which have evolved over the centuries along slightly different paths.

Man, the opportunist, would have thought of the wolf creature as a walking meal. His children might have found puppies but when they took them back to the cave to eat, they might have discovered that they were warm at night and playful companions, and domestication would have begun when both creatures became used to one another. Perhaps thousands of years would pass before man began to keep animals and to slowly change to a pastoral existence. The wolf/dog would still have hunted but by then man had discovered other facets of the animal which, by this time, was sharing his life. Man and dog became so dependent upon one another that each had an effect on the other's evolution. The mere fact that dogs guarded flocks and herds from predators would have made it easier for early man to develop. The fact that man provided regular food for the dog would change its development, too. Scientists have sufficient proof of the close proximity of the two species to satisfy themselves that dogs played an important role in primitive times.

## EARLY BREEDS

From Tomarctus came four distinct types of dog:
- The basic herding sheepdog
- Hunting, hauling and Toy dogs
- Sight hounds, e.g. Greyhounds and desert gaze hounds
- Large guarding Mastiff-style dogs and some water dogs

This is only a rough guide but all breeds of dogs stem from very few types; the incredible diversity of the canine race in both size and function is largely, but not altogether, derived from mankind's interference in the process of evolution. A Yorkshire Terrier is made exactly the same as a Great Dane; it comes from the same origins and has the same number of bones and muscles – the diminutive size comes from selective breeding.

## UNDERSTANDING YOUR DOG

To understand your own pet, even one as small as the Yorkshire Terrier, it is as well to know something of the dog in the wild. By nature the dog is a pack animal, a characteristic inherited from its wolf ancestors – not vast numbers of animals living together but rather extended family groups. They live within a clearly defined social pecking order with one dominant who can be either male or female. They are opportunists, not only killing their own prey with planned attacks but also scavenging food left by other predators, including things that we would consider disgusting. Their habits of eating faeces and rolling in objectionable muck stem from behavioural traits inherited from the wild state.

## Ancient Egypt

Hard evidence that dogs occupied a position of importance in early civilized society comes from ancient Egypt, some 6,000 years ago. Mummified remains of dogs were found in the tombs of kings indicating that they were the favourites of royalty. Anubis, a god who was half-man, half-dog, was believed to escort souls through limbo after death. Depicted on urns and vases of the time are recognisable gaze hounds, such as Greyhounds and Salukis. It is no surprise that hunting dogs should be in the forefront, but short-legged dogs are also depicted in the drawings of the period which may be the ancestors of terriers.

## Europe

In Europe, evidence of the popular use of dogs comes from Roman statues, mosaics and burial grounds, and archaeological digs in burial mounds have uncovered bones of dogs alongside human remains. There is evidence from carvings on tombstones, tapestries and paintings but it was not until 1570 that the first attempt to categorize dogs in print came with Dr Caius' book, *Of English Dogges*.

*Yorkies are naturally inquisitive and always ready for a game.*

## BEHAVIOURAL CHARACTERISTICS

Above all, the Yorkshire Terrier is a dog that loves his family; it is his pack. However, he has a streak of independence which all terriers have – after all, their original function was to do some relatively dangerous things on their own initiative. He is an easy dog to get on with, but he can be a little self-willed, sometimes trying to impose his will on others, especially the males. He adores to be involved with family happenings, and always wants to help. Provided that he is trained, the Yorkie is an excellent choice for a pet.

■ His dimunitive size makes him an ideal small dog and companion, but big enough to fit into any household.

■ He is sturdy and hardy, and will take exercise until his owner falls over.

Alternatively he will be content with short walks round the park.

■ Like most terriers, he understands children but toddlers should be taught to respect him because he might object to harsh treatment, although with babies he can be very protective.

■ By nature he is a happy dog, full of mischief, inquisitive, and always an amusing companion.

■ He is fairly easy to train and generally affable to other dogs although he will most certainly stand his ground if confronted.

■ He is not a noisy dog, but his big bark is out of proportion to his size, and he will guard the family home and warn of

*Yorkies can be suspicious of each other on first meeting.*

any visitors, welcome or otherwise.

■ He loves to give the impression that he is a very superior canine but underneath he is a softy, thriving on care and attention.

## Anti-social dogs

Problem dogs are invariably the fault of their owners; puppies, like children, have to be taught to behave. The problems usually start if the puppy is not socialized from birth. All puppies need to be handled and spoken to from the earliest possible age, the more the better, and whether they are pets or show dogs makes no difference. Dogs should not be treated as small hairy humans; they have their own special needs and only a thin veneer of domestication. In order to live satisfactorily in the human condition, they have to learn a language, the pattern of behaviour of a particular household and their position in the pack. Patient kindness, as with a young child, is the key. You do not expect a child to be potty-trained in a week, and nor should a puppy be expected to be house-trained in the same time.

A dog is always happiest when he knows his position relative to the other members of the family, and it is up to at least one person to train him, even if it is only basic stuff like 'sit', 'lie down' and 'come'. These three commands will stand you and your dog in good stead in most difficult situations. The dog will respect whoever trains him, providing it is done kindly and quietly on the 'praise and reward system' with the use of the voice. Never smack a Yorkshire Terrier; it is counter-productive, and you will end up with either a cowed dog or a mutinous one. In either case, he will be unhappy because in nature he is never struck – it will be beyond his understanding.

## Intelligence and senses

Dogs are intelligent animals, and they learn by short bursts of repetition – too much at one time and they become bored. Yorkies are bright and can easily think of something else which is more interesting to do, such as playing or running and imaginary hunting, but they respond well to training. Their senses are more acute than is often realised. They are quick to discern their owners' moods, and indeed they are so adept at reading body language that it is possible to think that they possess a sixth sense.

■ **Hearing**

Their hearing is probably between ten and twenty times more acute than that of humans. If they prick up their ears and bark, you can bet your life that there

*The Yorkie is an intelligent, energetic dog who loves a game and is always ready for a run in the garden, your local park or countryside.*

is something or someone around; you won't hear it but your dog will.

■ **Sense of smell**

The dog's most remarkable sense, and this applies to every breed, is its incredible sense of smell – expert estimates of this vary from 1,000 to 1,000,000 times more powerful than humans. Dogs can actually differentiate between one smell and dozens of others. Because of its hunting past, a Yorkie's sense of smell is highly developed, and there are cases of the bigger Yorkshire Terriers still hunting rabbits.

*To be socially acceptable, all dogs, even small ones such as Yorkshire Terriers, should be kept under control, especially in public places.*

## Dangerous dogs

It is incongruous to suggest that a Yorkshire Terrier is dangerous but the law does not differentiate between sizes of dogs. Neglect, harsh treatment and tormenting will eventually make most dogs dangerous to a degree, and even the comparatively small ones can bite from fear and a lack of security. A toy dog could inflict a nasty bite on a child if it were tormented enough.

Unfortunately, not everyone loves dogs, and there is an increasing anti-dog faction in society which delights in making life difficult for dog owners and seizing any excuse to discredit both owners and animals.

In 1991, after a couple of tragic incidents involving large dogs biting people, the British Government created new legislation, the Dangerous Dogs Act, ostensibly to rid the country of dogs bred to fight and those that they believed were most likely to attack human beings. They introduced a concept alien to the British sense of justice: the reversal of the burden of proof, meaning that, if accused, a dog was guilty under the Act before the trial and the only sentence on conviction was death.

Most people thought that only specified breeds would be affected but abuse of the Act showed quite clearly that any breed could be taken under different sections. In fact, a dog has only to frighten someone to be seized and to undergo court proceedings. There has even been a case of an elderly Pekinese being taken because its

barking frightened someone passing a stationary car.

Attitudes towards dogs are changing, and exaggerated media reports are designed to frighten people into believing that dogs are serious disease carriers when the truth is that ordinary hygiene will control the small risks. It behoves every dog owner to train his dog to be socially acceptable, never to allow him to walk unaccompanied and always to keep him under control in public places. Above all, the owner should pick up his dog's mess should he defecate in a public place. Most people find this habit repugnant and it is often the catalyst that stimulates the hatred and fear of dogs.

# PART TWO

# CARING FOR YOUR DOG

Buying any puppy or acquiring an adult dog is a huge responsibility, and caring for any dog will take up a lot of your time over the next ten or so years. Therefore it is not a decision to be taken lightly but one that requires careful consideration by all the members of your family. Small Yorkshire Terrier puppies can look especially appealing but they should never be bought on impulse. Many people forget that these cute little creatures need a lot of commitment and exercise. Yorkies make good companions and loving family pets but they are lively, intelligent dogs and require a lot of your attention. In this section on caring for your dog, you will find expert advice on choosing a puppy and looking after him; feeding, exercising and grooming your adult dog; breeding from your bitch; and how you can both enjoy the experience of showing your dog.

3

# ACQUIRING A PUPPY

## CHOOSING A PUPPY

This is one of the most important decisions a family has to take, as it will have the responsibility of a live creature for up to fifteen years. Dogs must not be regarded as objects to buy, sell or give away as the mood dictates. A dog is for life!

Before you embark on acquiring a dog, you should consider very carefully whether your lifestyle would permit you to take care of a puppy properly. This is particularly important if a husband and wife are working from early in the morning until early evening, in which case it is not possible or fair to introduce a puppy into the household. He would never develop his full potential; in fact, it could be courting disaster. The dog may develop behavioural problems, such as being destructive, antisocial and having dirty habits. Ask yourself the following questions and answer them honestly:

■ Can someone in the family always be relied upon to feed and exercise the dog regularly, and do the necessary grooming and training?

■ Is the upkeep affordable: not only the cost of food but also annual insurance premiums against sickness or sudden veterinary bills?

■ If the family travels abroad for holidays, consideration must be given to the dog – whether he has to stay in boarding kennels or stay with a trustworthy friend or relative. He must never be left alone in the house with food and water for as short a time as a weekend, nor should you rely upon neighbours to feed and exercise your dog in your absence. Are you prepared to pay for your dog to be looked after in kennels, or do you have a friend who would look after your dog properly?

### Buy from a licensed breeder

No puppy should be bought on impulse, so don't buy one from a man in a bar, a pet shop or a dealer – none of these will offer after-sales help or advice. They will probably disassociate themselves after the sale because almost certainly the puppy will not have been reared

*Take care when buying a Yorkie puppy; you should always go to a licensed breeder who specializes in this breed.*

correctly. There is even a danger that he will not be strong enough to survive. Indeed, he may require expensive veterinary treatment just to survive the first weeks after leaving the nursery.

Because of their popularity, Yorkshire Terriers are often bred by unscrupulous people out to make a quick buck, so you should also avoid commercial breeders and puppy farmers. The likelihood is that they only breed dogs for money and will not know nor care about the puppies' welfare or understand the problems of inherited conditions.

Buy from a licensed breeder who specializes in Yorkshire Terriers and is a dog show exhibitor, and who is approved by the Kennel Club or recommended by the Pro-Dogs charity, which has a system of vetting breeders and recommends only those who meet the highest standards. These breeders should have a 'buy back' guarantee in the event of the dog requiring re-homing for whatever reason. A guarantee effectively stops the dog falling into the wrong hands and perhaps being put down.

## Do your research

Having made the decision to buy a dog, find out as much as possible about the breed – your local library will help. The probability is that you will be looking for a puppy between the age of eight and ten weeks, and one of the first decisions you must make is which sex you want. There are merits for either, and you should ignore advice from non-experts, some of whom claim that male dogs are likely to be more difficult and are less faithful than gentler bitches. However, the truth is that there is little difference between the sexes, and dogs are what you train them to be. Remember that bitches need to be controlled when in season unless

they have been spayed; it is antisocial to have unwanted litters of pedigree pups and mongrel litters.

## Finding the right breeder

The Kennel Club will give you the telephone number of the secretary of one of the breed clubs, and you should speak to as many as possible. Tell them that you want a good representative of the breed. Do not buy a puppy just because he is cheap – remember that you are not just buying a puppy, you are buying years of experience. Find out when the breeders will be at a championship show within a reasonable distance of your home and arrange to meet. At the same time, look closely at the dogs in the ring, observing how the handlers treat their dogs. You may have to travel around but

be patient – the wait will be worthwhile. You will be looking for a breeder who cares, one who rears the puppies in the house and who will allow you to choose the one you want.

## Checklist

■ At the breeder's home, ask to see the mother with her litter.
■ Make sure that you keep your children under control. Just sit down quietly and watch the puppies.
■ Give them time to settle; they may not have seen many strangers.
■ The choice may be difficult. It may be that one pup will show interest in you but, in any event, you should look for a brave puppy who is full of himself.

## WHAT TO LOOK FOR IN A PUPPY

Make sure that the puppy moves freely and, for preference, has:
■ Black or nearly black pigmentation of the nose and eyelids.
■ Bright clean eyes and no discharges.
■ The colour of a Yorkshire Terrier puppy is not the same as that of an adult. He will be mainly black with tan feet, nose and bottom, but as he gets older the colours will change and appear in the right places.
■ Be suspicious if you are offered a puppy that is cheaper than its litter-mates because there is something wrong with him.
■ Take your time, and don't be pressurized into making a hasty decision; if you are not completely happy, don't buy one.

## The puppy's requirements

### 1 Bed and bedding

In his new home, the puppy should have a quiet corner allocated to him with a sturdy box or hard, unchewable plastic bed with some soft bedding – there are several almost indestructible, machine-washable, man-made fabrics available from pet shops.

### 2 Toys and chews

Your puppy will need a couple of strong toys, an artificial bone and some hide chews that he can chew on; like a child, he will need something to bite whilst he is teething. Everything should be unbreakable and large enough not to swallow.

### 3 An escape-proof garden

This is a necessity as puppies can get through surprisingly small holes. A wire mesh fence about 1.2 m (4 ft) high would be sufficient, with gates that do not stay open if visiting tradesmen forget to close them. It is not that puppies want to get

## BUYING A PUPPY

■ The best breeders will include one month's insurance in the price or offer facilities or advice on insurance.

■ They should give you a diet sheet and a few days' supply of the food on which the puppy has been reared; this will prevent any tummy upsets. Get in a supply of the food he's used to, and if you change it for any reason make the change over a period of time by adding new food to the original, gradually increasing the proportion of the new one.

■ The puppy should have been wormed fully in the light of modern knowledge, and advice given for further treatment.

■ Kennel Club registration documents and a pedigree should be handed over on completion of the sale with a receipt.

■ Be prepared to answer a few forthright questions; the best breeders are concerned that their puppies go to good homes.

away but they do have an insatiable curiosity, and they do not realise that your neighbours will not appreciate a small dog rampaging over their flower beds. Dogs don't know the difference between flowers and weeds, so do not be surprised if your puppy offers you your own geraniums because he thinks he's doing you a favour. Another important point to remember is that puppies do not have any traffic sense; if they run free on the road, the chances are that they will be run over by a car.

## Collecting the puppy

At least two people should collect the new puppy, and he should travel back home on the passengers' knees. He will need a lot of affection and comforting. Just think, he may never have been in a car before and he will be separated from his family for the first time. Take some tissues, a towel and a little water as he may be travel sick or thirsty. Do not put him out of the car at lay-bys, as these are serious sources of infection and he will still have to finish his course of vaccinations.

## BRINGING THE PUPPY HOME

### At home

Back at home let your puppy's first day be quiet and peaceful. Give the newcomer time to explore, give him a name, be with him, talk to him and play gently with him – he shouldn't be harassed in any way. This is an important training period, and what you do now will set the pattern for his future behaviour. For example, some modern behaviourists advocate not permitting a puppy to sit on the furniture in case he gets ideas above his station, but I live with several dogs and I let them sit where they like – they soon get off if I want the seat!

### At night

■ The first few nights may present problems for you and your puppy, so surround his box with newspaper in case he wants to urinate.

46

■ Put a well-covered hot water bottle in the bed and leave a radio playing all night. It is not kind to let the puppy cry and howl all through the night.

■ He will be lonely, and some dogs don't like  being left on their own at all, so it is not unknown for new owners to sleep in the same room downstairs with the puppy. Some allow him to sleep in his bed by the side of their bed – a hand touching him is a comfort. However, it is definitely not a good idea to allow him to sleep in your bed.

■ If you don't want him to go upstairs, fix a childproof gate at the bottom. If he does go upstairs with you, carry him up and down; if he falls downstairs he is likely to injure himself severely – he is very small and his bones will not be set until he reaches about six months.

## Veterinary services

Check the vets in your neighbourhood, and find one with whom you can get along. Talk to him about your new Yorkie puppy, and be guided by him as far as vaccination and worming are concerned.

### ■ Worming

Buy your worming preparation from the vet and follow the instructions carefully. Even if your puppy has been wormed regularly by the breeder, he is likely to have round worms, and you will need to

## INSURANCE

Dogs are most vulnerable to disease as puppies or veterans, and it is wise to have a health and accident insurance because of the ever-escalating costs of veterinary services. Several reputable companies offer different levels of cover, and details can be obtained from the breeder, the Kennel Club, your vet or from advertisements in the canine press. Diminutive though they are, Yorkshire Terriers are a hardy breed and you may never see a vet except for vaccination purposes, but should it prove necessary you will be glad you had the foresight to take out insurance.

*Vaccinate your puppy against the most common infectious diseases.*

administer the drug within two weeks of acquiring him. Dispose of the faeces down the toilet or burn them; simple hygiene will prevent any infections spreading to the family or to the public.

### ■ Vaccination

Modern vaccines are almost 100 per cent effective. Distemper and parvovirus are still killer diseases, and between eight and ten weeks of age the puppy is unlikely to have been vaccinated. He will have only a vestige of antibodies left for countering these diseases, and should not go out until the vet approves it for fear of infection. First vaccinations will be at about twelve weeks and the boosters two weeks later, after which he'll be virtually safe from infection. Keep the certificate in a safe

YORKIES AND CHILDREN

Instruct the children that the dog's bed is his private sanctuary, and when he wants to sleep he must be allowed to do so without disturbance. Just as a baby needs sleep for growing purposes, so does a puppy. Yorkies generally get along well with children but no puppy can be expected to suffer pain, however accidentally, at the hands of youngsters. He will not know, nor care, that it is accidental, and he knows only one method of retaliation or defence: a nip with sharp teeth. A well-socialized puppy will bite only as a last resort when he is either hurt or frightened. Anyway, you will find that the children will live at a higher level than the puppy who will enjoy dragging about the clothes that they leave on the floor. Their tapes and other things they value will be chews to him, so he may teach them something!

place; you will need it if your dog ever goes to a boarding kennel.

## Knowing his way home

Until his vaccinations are complete, you can familiarize the puppy with the local geography by carrying him around. This will help him to get used to heavy traffic without putting him down. Don't worry too much about exercising him for the first six months; his normal activities of playing and running in the house and garden will be quite sufficient. When he is able to go out, make sure you show him all the routes leading back to your house. This easy procedure will help him if he ever gets lost.

## FEEDING

The weekly bill to feed a Yorkshire Terrier properly is relatively inexpensive, but he does need high-quality food. At eight weeks old, a puppy's stomach is probably no bigger than a large marble, but he will still require small quantities of nutritious food six times a day, together with a continuous supply of clean water.

■ Follow the instructions on the diet sheet or on the food packets.

■ Feed the best food, always at the same time and in the same place but not direct from the refrigerator. It should be at room temperature or lukewarm.

■ Do not leave the food down for too long in case flies contaminate it.

■ Do not allow your puppy to eat the cat's food and neither should the cat and dog be fed together.

■ Some dogs react unfavourably to cow's milk, so check with the breeder if your puppy is used to it. If not, don't risk it – he can live and prosper on water.

■ As the puppy gets older, the meals will get less in number but larger in quantity until at the age of between six and eight months, he will be eating two meals a day.

■ It is not wise to feed dogs with titbits from the table. If you don't start, they won't bother you. They put on weight easily if they are greedy, and a fat dog is unhealthy. Train the children not to give the puppy sweets, sugar-based biscuits or cakes. He will eat them but they're not good for him.

### Supplements

If good proprietary food, such as canned meat with wholemeal biscuit, or a complete diet food is used it will be

scientifically balanced and there will be no need for any vitamin or mineral supplements. If you mix your own, it probably won't be balanced, but the amounts of additional supplements must be carefully considered, because too much or too little can easily upset a puppy's development. If you are unsure, seek veterinary advice.

The most common health hazard in the puppy is diarrhoea, which can be caused by the simple changing of water or a sudden change of diet. Take him off all dairy products, change the food and feed only boiled rice and chicken. If there is no improvement in twenty-four hours, take him to the vet.

## Training your puppy

Contrary to some beliefs, a puppy is never too young to start the training process, as long as it's done with gentle firmness and lavish praise and reward when it goes right. There are four areas in which both the owner and puppy can benefit from an early start. These are as follows:

- Toilet-training
- Lead-training
- Grooming
- Basic obedience

### TOILET-TRAINING YOUR PUPPY

Leave quantities of newspaper down on the floor, making it easily accessible, and when he uses it, gradually make it smaller. When it's down to one sheet, move it short distances nightly towards the door. Then when it's by the door, it's easy to put it on the step. Just be careful not to leave the paper you are reading on the floor by your armchair at night!

## Toilet-training

When a puppy wishes to urinate or defecate he will invariably do the same thing: he may turn around in circles, he may run backwards and forwards or he may go to the same spot each time. It is up to you to be aware of this and, when he goes into his act, to interrupt and put him outside. Wait for him to perform, praise him and call him back into the house.

Get into a routine, and put him out at the same times, such as when he gets up in the morning, after every meal, after every period of rest and before he settles down for the night. Always wait and praise him after the performance. By all means, grumble at him if he does it in the house but only if you actually interrupt him in the process. Shouting at him after the event will achieve nothing; he won't connect it with the deed, and as defecation is natural, he will not relate his natural functions with punishment. Rubbing his nose in his mess means nothing – it's probably more unpleasant for you than it is for him! Hitting him won't train him, nor should you preface grumbling or shouting with his name. When he's young, you must make him associate his name with pleasant things.

## LEAD-TRAINING

1 Buy a cat collar and a light lead for your puppy. Put the collar on during the day, and take it off at night. He'll get used to wearing it very quickly.

2 After a couple of days, attach the lead and let it trail on the ground until he ignores it. Keep an eye on him, and don't let him get tangled up – this may take a day or two.

3 Then pick up the lead and let him walk about, going where he pleases, but at the same time assert a little pressure. Try this several times during the day.

4 When he's ready, holding the lead, draw him gently towards you calling his name. When he gets to you, award him with a tiny piece of fried liver or his favourite titbit and praise him. Very soon he'll walk happily beside you – just don't let him pull.

## GROOMING

Because of the type of coat the adult Yorkie grows, it is vital to get him used to being groomed when young.

■ Start by putting him on your lap or standing him on a table and brushing and combing him gently in the direction the hair lies. He'll play-bite the brush and probably spring about but it won't hurt him, so ignore it and eventually he will stop. He'll be standing still after a few days so be patient. When later, he might have to be scissored and prepared for showing, this early work will pay dividends.

■ Unless he wallows in muck, there's no need to bath the Yorkie often; regular brushing will remove the dirt.

## Basic obedience

1 **Teaching your dog to sit** Start by teaching your puppy to sit and come on command. To teach him to sit, apply a little gentle pressure on his back by the tail with one hand while lifting gently under the throat with the other. Say the word 'sit' regularly. Do this a few times twice a day, and soon he'll obey and sit on command.

2 **Teaching your dog to come** After your Yorkie has become used to the collar and light lead, attach a long cord, 4-5 m (12-15 ft) long, or use one of the modern lightweight extending leads.

■ Starting from about 1 m (3 ft) away, tell him to 'sit'. Keep a small piece of fried liver or some other titbit

concealed in your other hand.

■ Wait a few seconds and call him by name, adding the word 'here'. He'll ignore you, but tempt him forwards with the reward of the liver or titbit.

■ Gradually extend the distance at the end of the cord, still commanding him to sit, and then calling and rewarding him.

■ When giving him his reward,

hold it in front of him. If you feed from a height, he will spend his time looking up at you and for showing purposes this will give him a disastrous outline. Five minutes twice a day are all that is needed to teach your dog to come to you. Keep it light-hearted and don't persist with this type of training if he is tired and not in the mood.

# CHAPTER FOUR

# THE ADULT DOG

## TRAINING AND TRAVELLING

If you have followed the advice in the preceding chapters, by the time your Yorkie reaches adulthood he should be trained at least in the fundamentals and should be under control. I do not mean by 'control' that the dog should be subdued. On the contrary, he should have all the playfulness and exuberance expected of the breed. Mischief is a by-word for the Yorkshire Terrier and this happy state of affairs should last into old age.

The Yorkie is not known for successful formal obedience training or agility, and very few terriers or toy breeds are trained in this way. However, there's no reason why they shouldn't compete. The obstacles are smaller and the distances shorter, and in America many small breeds have reached high levels in competition.

When a little dog goes to a training session, he is sometimes met with incredulity from owners of German Shepherds and Border Collies who consider their dogs to be the only ones worth competing with. However, perseverance will produce results although, occasionally, the terrier types will create an independent run if only to amuse themselves, but, after all, they are not serious dogs.

### Training classes

■ Whichever training classes you choose, it is important that the tutors should use modern gentle methods. Harsh training and punishments are a thing of the past and, with patient care, your dog will be a credit to you and his breed.

■ Be sure to reinforce the training at home. In the initial stages, your dog is likely to forget rather quickly, and once-a-week training is not enough.

■ Clubs fall into several categories, and the pet owner wanting a well-behaved dog should seek a general training club, making sure that they teach domestic obedience or the Good Companion scheme. Other clubs specialize in teaching both owners and dogs the skills of dog showing, basic obedience, training and agility. All types are

*Yorkshire Terriers are full of mischief; however, with patience and care they can be trained in the fundamentals.*

social occasions and bring together all sorts of people with a common interest.

## Rescued and older dogs

It is sometimes possible to buy a dog of between six and twelve months old. Breeders may, as they say, 'run one on', meaning that they keep a dog to see if he develops well enough for showing, and if he doesn't make the grade he will be found a home. This does not mean that there is anything seriously wrong with the dog, only that something is not quite right for showing purposes. It may be the set of the ears or a misplaced tooth but if the buyer has no intention of showing or breeding, there is no reason why such a dog shouldn't be considered.

The positive side is that the new owner will not go through the work associated with caring for and training a puppy, but on the negative side the young dog may not have been schooled in the way another owner wants, he may have unwanted characteristics and it will take time, patience and expertise to get it right.

■ The same problems may occur with a rescued dog. Note that there is a difference between rescued and re-homed dogs. Several of the major welfare societies will take in stray and unwanted dogs, and these can include pedigree animals. After vetting them, most will try to home them within a week or two.

### TRAINING CLUBS AND CLASSES

There are many training clubs for puppies and older dogs which are run by enthusiastic dog people. They are usually advertised in the local press, but you can also find out about them by enquiring at your veterinary surgery or police station. In the UK, the Kennel Club will advise on clubs operating their 'Good Companion' scheme, which enables owners to teach their dogs simple obedience in order that they can fit into society. Upon the successful conclusion of this course, a certificate is awarded to the dog and owner.

In most cases, they are not aware of the reason for the dogs not being wanted; they may be biters or barkers, and there's no way of finding this out unless you live with them. A rescued dog may have been the victim of cruelty or neglect, in which case it takes a lot of loving care to get them right but it is worthwhile.

■ Yorkshire Terriers are fortunate in that they have a very good breed rescue which is a re-homing service, and they often know why the dog has ended up in their care. If not, they try to find out. The unfortunate dog can be in their hands because of divorce, the death of the owner or some other unavoidable circumstance. The breed rescues will take the dog in, have it vetted, pay for any veterinary treatment

and keep the dog long enough to find out whether there are any problems. They will investigate anyone who wants one of their dogs to ensure that the dog goes to a good home. In these cases, it is possible to find a trained dog who will make a fine, trouble-free addition

*A rescued Yorkie can reward you with loyalty and companionship.*

to the family. Normally they will not come with papers so they cannot be bred from with the subsequent puppies registered with the Kennel Club.

## Travel

From a very young age, a dog should be trained to travel in a car. If he is sick, you must try to make a car journey an enjoyable experience.

■ Play with him in the car when it is at a standstill for ten minutes a day for two or three days.

■ Do the same for the next three days with the engine running.

■ Move the car slowly for a hundred yards for a few days, and feed him in the car.

■ When you finally take him some distance, always drive to a place where he can enjoy himself, such as a park or a field, and eventually he should associate car travel with pleasure.

## Caution

■ It is vital that no dog should be left in a car in the sun because the interior temperatures can rise astonishingly in a short time and the dog can die in a few minutes even with the windows open.

■ Remembering that a Yorkie can wriggle through a three-inch gap, be careful. It is not really safe to drive with loose dogs in the car, and sudden stoppages or accidents can cause a dog to be flung through the windscreen or suffer injury inside the car. Television advertisements have shown how a puppet child can be flung through a car windscreen impacted at 50 kph (30 mph). The same would happen to a loose dog.

## Travel boxes

It is acknowledged that the best and safest way for a dog to travel is in a travel box. This prevents him being thrown about by the movement of the vehicle and give him a sense of security. In an accident, it is not unusual for rear doors and tailgates to fly open, throwing loose dogs into the road and putting them at risk from overtaking traffic. Sometimes they are so terrified that they disappear into the distance never to be found. A travel box will prevent this happening.

■ Dog guards to confine dogs are made for most makes of car. Specially made cages fitting the shape of the modern estate car's sloping back are also available, which effectively keep the dog safer.

■ It is not cruel to put a dog into a box; in fact, he enjoys the privacy. The box or cage can be used as an indoor kennel providing it is of the correct size, about 30 cm (12 in) wide, 40 cm (16 in) high and 50 cm (20 in) long, allowing plenty of room for the dog to lie full length and stretch out.

■ Train the dog to go into the box by feeding him inside it with the door open for a few days, then shut the door for a few minutes. Finally, leave the door shut for about an hour. This is very useful training if you want to go shopping for an hour or so, or need to restrain the dog for a few minutes. Do not over-use this device in the home; your dog will get bored and he does like to be with his family. Also, you do want him to warn you of unwelcome visitors.

**Note:** There is a little point of danger when taking a lively dog out in the car. When you stop and open the door, he is likely to jump out like lightning, so this is where your 'sit' training is invaluable. When the car stops, command him to sit and wait, open the door and only let him out when you are ready. This gives you time to put on his lead.

## FEEDING

As with a puppy, you should continue feeding high-quality food at the same time each day to an adult dog. When a dog's stomach is full he is liable to be less watchful than when it is empty, so giving a dog his main meal in the morning will make him more watchful at night, whereas a night-fed dog will sleep more soundly.

### Convenience foods

If it is true that we are what we eat, then so are dogs. They are remarkable creatures and can subsist on virtually any food, but in order to be healthy and long lived they need a balanced diet, containing the right amounts of protein, vitamins, fibre and fat. Off-the-shelf convenience pet foods are a fast-growing industry. Apart from the obvious benefits, the major manufacturers have nutrition scientists researching our pets' dietary needs and formulating feedstuffs with every contingency in mind.

### Protein content

■ Pet owners need to be aware that certain foods suit certain dogs, especially as modern dog food marketing has convinced many people that the higher the protein value, the better the food. This is not so, and too much protein is as damaging as too little. If your Yorkie is a high-activity animal who runs miles each day and hunts rabbits, he will need a food that is high in protein. However, if he is your average pet, playing in the garden chasing a ball and having a couple of short walks each day, he does not. All prepared dog foods have their protein content written on the packaging, and the average Yorkshire Terrier needs around fifteen per cent protein in the manufacturer's terms. There are foods to suit all sizes and all activities, the suitability of which is plainly marked on the packets. If you feed your dog with your own home-cooked food, you should be careful when offering any additional supplements. Too much or too little will harm the dog, and veterinary guidance should be sought.

■ Too high a protein value can cause skin problems in most dogs; unless checked and diagnosed, these can be serious conditions. Any sign of changes in the skin colour or texture, or any sore spot on your Yorkie and you should consult the vet immediately. He will probably recommend changing your dog's diet to a chicken and rice combination or one that is low in protein. All dairy products should be stopped and strictly no human food treats like cake and biscuits given. It has been found that dogs benefit by the addition of oil in their diet; one capsule of cod liver oil or a teaspoon of olive oil or corn oil two or three times a week helps with skin and hair condition. The major petfood companies have advisory departments which exist solely to solve their customers' problems, so get in touch if the need arises.

## How many meals?

Controversy as to whether to feed two meals or one meal a day has raged for hundreds of years. My view is that we don't like to be hungry, and neither does a dog, so I feed my dogs their main meal in the morning and a snack in the evening. The only treats that dogs should have are dog food based, biscuit bonios and edible chews. Bones of any description should not be fed. The reasons are that cooked chop and chicken bones split into jagged pieces and can pierce the stomach lining. Some people advocate the use of big marrow bones, but beware. Dogs' jaws and teeth,

even the smallest, are so strong that they can crumble the bone and swallow it. Over a period of time it can get trapped and become impacted in the digestive tract and has to be removed in a fairly major operation with the attendant dangers. The second reason for not feeding bones is that some dogs get mega possessive over a big juicy bone and become ferocious in its defence. Children and other dogs can be challenged unless the dog has been trained to give up his food, and even then he may only give it up to the person he considers to be the pack leader. It's better not to give him any temptation. If the dog is destined for the show ring, bones of any description will ruin the face hair, and to keep the teeth clean, hard dog biscuits will be just as effective as will hide chews which are easily available from pet stores.

# NEUTERING

There is an on-going discussion on the merits of neutering pet dogs and bitches. With permission from the Kennel Club, it is possible to show neutered dogs but purists argue that there is no point in winning with excellent dogs if they cannot reproduce themselves.

■ Bitches come into season from six months old and thence about twice a year, with variations, into old age. There is a view that bitches should be allowed to have at least one litter, which, it is said, will prevent them from having infections of the womb later in life.

■ The in-season bitch will attract the attentions of all the males that get her scent and she must be kept in isolation for around three weeks or until it is over. If not, she may be mated by any stray dog and produce a litter of mongrels which will probably increase the stray dog problem and overload the services of canine welfare charities. In the case of a small Yorkie, the puppies may be too big to be born properly and her life could be in jeopardy. It is antisocial to have a litter of unwanted puppies so avoid it.

■ If the bitch becomes pregnant accidentally the vet can stop it with one injection if caught soon enough. It is possible to stop the season chemically and, again, the vet can supply a course of tablets which, if started in time, will prevent the onset of her season. However, this is not always satisfactory because it can induce side effects.

■ To really have peace of mind, surgical neutering is the only realistic option. Always make the decision in consultation with your vet. The spaying operation is routine and your bitch will recover from the anaesthetic a few hours later and will return to normal very quickly. The benefits are that she will never come into season again and will never suffer another false pregnancy.

■ Sometimes the act of neutering either a dog or bitch will cause the coat characteristics to change, softening and thickening. There is some evidence that both sexes tend to put on weight after the operation, and therefore more careful control of the diet is needed.

■ Some vets and behaviourists believe the castration of a dominant male will alter its character and stop any further aggression. This is open to question, and there is no proof that instincts and thought processes undergo a change. You may feel the difference knowing that you are not contributing to the problems of canine over-population. The operation is very simple, and the dog will recover in a couple of days.

## EXERCISE

To be healthy and happy, the adult Yorkie needs exercise and things to do. He is an active, inquisitive dog and can get by on a minimum of exercise but to be in good condition he needs free running and play. He can be taught easily to retrieve a ball, and half an hour a day in the garden throwing a ball will keep him in hard, muscular condition.

Give him things to tax his mind: you can hide the ball and let him find it, or throw it into thick vegetation – the more contact you have, the happier he'll be.

In towns and cities, two short walks a day on the lead are probably all that is needed. Make a point of never letting your dog off the lead in public places or near busy roads as the Yorkie has so curious a nature that if something attracts his notice he'll run off, oblivious of your entreaties, and if he crosses a road he risks his life. A 5m (15 ft) extending lead is useful as it gives him an illusion of freedom and the handler stays in control.

He should be trained to defecate on your own property but dogs can make mistakes, so be sure to carry something to enable you to pick up the mess should his mistake be on public land. Things are better in the country but if you go onto farming land he must not be allowed near livestock, especially sheep, as a farmer is legally entitled to shoot a dog if he believes it to be a threat to his animals and it won't worry him if it is a small dog.

*Make sure you give your Yorkie enough exercise and running to keep him fit, happy and healthy.*

## BOARDING KENNELS

The quality of boarding kennels varies and unless you have been recommended to one in particular you should call on two or three to check them out. Rates will vary and, in general, the more they offer the greater the cost.

Visit some kennels and and ask to be shown around. Look for clean, sweet-smelling quarters with dogs' toys lying around and soft bedding. Once you have settled on one, discuss the feeding, making sure they understand any special needs of your pet. Get a quote for the amount it is likely to cost.

When leaving your dog at a kennels, it is a good idea to leave a used sweater with him so that your scent will be a comfort in your absence. It is surprising how most dogs will settle into boarding kennels if the staff are sympathetic. Ask them which vet services their kennels and assure yourself that they will not hesitate to call on him should the need arise. Meanwhile, make sure the insurance is paid up.

Good kennels will expect up-to-date inoculation certificates on arrival against the main infectious diseases. It is advisable to add a vaccination against kennel cough, this being one condition that kennels find difficult to counter. It is not normally a killer disease in adult animals but one that will make life uncomfortable for the dog and worrying

for the owner. Finally, if your return date is delayed, let the kennels know as soon as possible – they need to manipulate available space.

## Alternatives to kennels

The alternative to boarding kennels when you go on holiday is to leave your dog with relations or friends. Many will like the idea but danger lurks. Ideally, the dog should be introduced to the household and its area before leaving him. The people to whom you are entrusting your Yorkie should love and understand dogs and, for preference, have no other pet in the house.

Make a list of the dog's requirements to leave with your friends, and buy his food in advance before you go away. Above all, you must be sure that they fulfil some demanding criteria before you entrust your pet to them. Accidents do happen and you won't have any recourse against your friends except through the courts. Good boarding kennels will normally meet their legal obligations because they value their business.

## Adult vaccination and worming

To maintain the antibody levels against the five main diseases of canine distemper, canine parvovirus, infectious canine hepatitis, leptospirosis and kennel cough, it is necessary for your Yorkshire Terrier to have annual booster

### IDENTIFICATION

In a public place, at all times, the law requires your dog to have identification on the collar. This should bear your name and address with the telephone number. Do not engrave it with the dog's name; there's no point in helping dog thieves. On the reverse side, it is suggested that the word 'Reward' appears. This often helps to get your dog returned if he gets lost, especially if children find him.

vaccinations. Your vet will usually send a reminder when they are due.

■ Regular worming, usually to control roundworms, must be part of the routine. Not only is it necessary from the family's health point of view but also from the dog's. A worm infestation will adversely affect his condition: he will look poorly, his coat will have a lank and unhealthy appearance and he may suffer skin disorders. In extreme cases, a dog can die of worm infestation. It is a fact that bitches harbour more worm larvae in an inert state in their bodies than dogs. The larvae are activated with the hormonal changes occurring when the bitch comes into season or becomes pregnant. Because of the ease with which dogs can re-infect themselves the vet will probably recommend worming three or four times a year for adult dogs.

## DIFFICULT DOGS

If you follow my recommendations for socializing your puppy and train him from an early age, your dog should not be difficult but, allowing for a dog's natural instinct and his heritage, you cannot expect a Yorkshire Terrier to behave like a human being. He will behave as he is: a dog with an independent spirit, a little terrier.

There are two main reasons why some dogs can be difficult.

■ The first, quite simply, is incorrect training and handling from an early age and this can be blamed on the owner. Obviously the owner cannot correct the dog's behaviour because he created it in the first place, and a veterinary surgeon would refer such an owner to a dog behaviourist who would teach the dog better manners. However, the owner too should learn how to handle the dog because unless the new training is reinforced, the dog will revert to his original behaviour. A good trainer at a club should be able to correct faulty behaviour, particularly if he has watched the dog since he was young.

■ The second reason is that there is a remote possibility that the dog is slightly insane. If it happens with humans, it can happen with dogs and an afflicted animal will require a lot of patience and understanding.

## GROOMING

There are two levels of grooming a Yorkshire Terrier: the pet level and the show level. The growth, maintenance and preparation of a show coat is a specialist's job, which requires extensive study and practice. The majority of pet Yorkshire Terriers are kept with a short haircut, cut to 7.5 cm (3 in) or 10 cm (4 in) over the whole body with very sharp scissors. The topknot is tied in a ribbon to prevent any hair getting into the eyes.

Haircutting need be done only every four months or so but, because the dog does not moult, care should be taken to keep the coat tangle free by simple combing for a few minutes daily. Even with a short coat, little knots and tangles can occur in particular spots, such as under the front legs, the underneath generally and behind the ears.

Train the puppy to lie on your lap on his back with the head towards you. Gently tease out the knots with your fingertips and remove the loose bits with a steel comb. Then place him on a table and gently comb the rest of the body, holding him firmly to prevent him either falling or jumping off. Eyes and ears should be examined at this time and kept clean. For obvious reasons, the bottom should be kept free of hair.

*Start your grooming session by combing the trouble spots on the head where knots and tangles need to be teased out gently. Tie back the topknot with a ribbon to keep the long hair out of the dog's eyes.*

If the coat is neglected and allowed to grow long, it will matt and tangle. In severe cases it is impossible to tease out the knots and it's painful for the dog, so sometimes the only answer is to cut the matted hair off down to the skin. The dog is so small that it only takes a few minutes to keep him looking and feeling good, so make grooming a regular and enjoyable part of your daily routine together.

Top left: keep the hair on the feet tangle-free for comfort.

Top right: gentle brushing helps to keep the long hair of the coat straight. If you do not show your dog, you may wish to trim the body hair and keep it short for easy everyday care and maintenance.

Above: although grooming a Yorkie with a show coat can take considerable time, it should be an enjoyable experience for you and your dog.

# THE SHOW DOG

*Great care must be taken when introducing crackers for the first time. The hair must not be pulled or your dog may never accept the procedure. Initially, he may scratch them off and you may have to patiently replace them many times before he grows accustomed to wearing them (see page 90).*

## BATHING YOUR DOG

Anti-flea shampoo is easily available if your dog has fleas, but it is not necessary to bathe a pet Yorkie very often. There are dry shampoos but regular brushing should keep him clean. Only specially formulated dog shampoo should be used or a human baby shampoo, and in all cases the eyes should be protected. Make sure he is thoroughly rinsed and dry before he goes out; Yorkies are hardy but dampness for a period of time is not good.

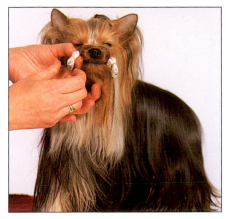

## EXAMINING YOUR DOG

*To keep your dog in good health, you should examine him regularly. Look closely at his eyes and keep them clean with a veterinary eye-wipe or some damp cotton wool – do this very carefully so as not to hurt him.*

*The ears can be a source of infection and you should examine them regularly. There should be no visible wax or an unpleasant smell.*

## PARASITES

An unkempt coat attracts parasites, such as fleas. Free-ranging cats and hedgehogs carry fleas and ticks which could infest the cleanest dog. Don't buy any old flea spray off the shelf; some of them are toxic, especially to puppies, so ask your vet who will have the appropriate treatment. As well as treating your dog, you must spray the bedding and its surrounds to break the life cycle of the flea.

*Left: lift the lips to look at your dog's teeth. They should be white and smooth. Below: clip the claws carefully to avoid cutting the sensitive quick.*

# CHAPTER FIVE

# BREEDING

## RESPONSIBLE BREEDING AND MATING

Some real thought must be given to the breeding of Yorkshire Terriers before you embark on this course; breeding dogs to earn some extra cash for, say, a video camera or a holiday is not good enough reason. Not only will you be bringing puppies into the world for which you must accept responsibility but also you are entering the realms of the breed fancy extending back over one hundred years. You should not breed dogs if your motivation is anything other than the wish to breed excellent specimens for the furtherance of that breed.

In the UK, there are laws governing the breeding of dogs, and should you have two or more breeding bitches, you will require a breeder's licence for which you should apply to your local council. The sale of dogs also comes under the Consumer Acts, and should there be complaints by any person buying a puppy from you concerning its suitability for the purpose they bought it, it will be necessary to show that you have taken advice and have bred the litter taking into consideration all known genetic factors, and acted in good faith.

### The novice breeder

The Yorkie is one of the most popular of all breeds and, as a result, is subject to the 'get rich' commercial breeders who have no consideration or understanding of genetics and are probably guilty of introducing hereditary anomalies and puppies of inferior quality. The genuine fancier may take years to breed out the problems created by ignorant breeders. Caring properly for a litter is expensive and time consuming, and requires privacy for the bitch – the new family should not be left for long periods.

Knowledge is the key to successful and responsible breeding, so begin by reading everything available on the breed. You could consult the breeder of your own bitch, providing he/she is recognised as being successful and is held in esteem by other breeders. Most breeders will help the novice all through the various stages, starting with advice as to which stud dog is suitable for that particular bitch through to the sale of the puppies.

*The puppy's coat colour changes and gets lighter as he grows older.*

One problem that is peculiar to breeders of Yorkshire Terriers is having to contend with the possibility that large puppies can be born of small bitches, causing birth difficulties that end with Caesarean sections. Because both parents are small does not mean necessarily that the puppies will also be small, and without knowledge of the line great damage can be done to the bitch and the breed. Consultation with established breeders is essential for the novice.

## Stud dogs

You may think that any stud dog will impregnate a bitch – true, but will the resultant puppies be of sufficient standard? The stud lines must match the bitch lines and this type of information can come only from people experienced in the breed. Make certain the chosen dog is properly registered with the Kennel Club because if this is not the case, his puppies cannot be registered or exhibited.

A fee must be paid to the stud owner at the completion of a mating; the amount varies but it should be agreed between both parties at the onset. Usually it covers two services in the same season by the same dog. Remember that it is for the mating and not for the results. If no puppies result from the union, most bona fide breeders will offer the next mating free of charge, but this is a concession, not a rule. Some breeders will loan out bitches in return for puppies, which is not a good idea and often ends in the courts. Full agreement of all facets of the loan must be agreed in writing; there is a Kennel Club agreement available and it is wise to use it.

An experienced stud owner will manage the mating without problems if the bitch is ready. The mating itself should be easy with no stress for either animal; forced matings are not advisable and there should be no need to muzzle the bitch. A 'tie' in which both dogs are tied together for anything from ten minutes to an hour is natural and preferred although not entirely necessary as the semen passes from dog to bitch within the first twenty seconds or so. The reason for the tie is unknown. The stud owner will give the bitch owner a signed Kennel Club form as confirmation of the mating, the date and the dog used, together with a receipt for the money paid.

## The bitch

She should not be bred from at the first season and neither should she have puppies after the age of eight years if the litter is to be registered with the Kennel Club. A further restriction is that it is not considered advisable to have litters from consecutive seasons. Make sure that the bitch's vaccinations are up to date because you want the puppies to have plenty of antibodies at birth. It is necessary also that the bitch should be wormed. However, it is possible to worm her during pregnancy after taking veterinary advice.

The scientific term for a 'season' is 'oestrus', and a bitch will come into season about twice a year. This varies considerably within the breed, and it may be three times in two years.

■ The first sign is a bloody discharge from the vulva which, in anything from nine to eleven days, will change to a straw colour when the bitch is ready for mating. It must be emphasised that the timing will vary with each bitch and each season.

■ Another sign of readiness is when the tail twitches from side to side if slight pressure is asserted near the tail with the dog in a standing position.

■ The signs should be carefully monitored because the period of time during which the bitch will conceive is limited. A vet can do tests to determine the ideal time for mating but, overall, the dogs know best.

**Note:** It is usual for the bitch to be taken to the dog for mating, but distance should not come into the equation as the aim is to find the most suitable stud dog.

# PREGNANCY

After the mating, the bitch should be taken home quietly and treated as usual. There are subtle signs that she is pregnant:

■ She may be quieter than usual.

■ Her teats may increase in size.

■ She may have a colourless discharge after two or three weeks.

The period of gestation varies from sixty to sixty-six days with the average being sixty three. If the bitch shows any evidence of stress or pain, consult the vet.

## Whelping preparation

In the last week before the birth, prepare a room, which ideally should be heated to 18-22°C (70-75°F), in which the bitch can have peace without disturbance by children or other animals.

■ You will need a whelping box, which is capable of being closed but is well ventilated, with a door for the bitch with a flap at the base to ensure that the puppies cannot fall out or follow her when they begin to walk.

■ Pig rails should be fitted around the inside four walls, and set 7.5 cm (3 in) above the floor to prevent the bitch rolling on her young. The puppies should be able to squeeze under them for safety.

■ Ideally it would be around 75 x 50 x 50 cm (30 x 20 x 20 in) high. This would allow

### DETECTING PREGNANCY

Many novices want to know as soon as possible whether the bitch is pregnant and how many puppies she will have. Ultra-sound scanning is the only reliable method of establishing this but puppies can only be detected at the correct time. Some people can palpate the bitch, and, by feeling very gently, the heads can be counted during the period between the twenty-first and twenty-eighth day. Veterinary blood tests will detect pregnancy but not the number of puppies. Later in the pregnancy, the movement of puppies can be seen and felt.

the mother to move freely and stretch out, both of which are important when suckling a litter of puppies.

■ A box of this size will prevent the puppies from straying too far from their mates and suffering from cold; the correct temperature is vital to their growth and well-being.

■ Some breeders use an infra-red heater hanging on chains, and care must be exercised with the height adjustment – too close may burn the bitch's back. I prefer to use an aluminium heating pad under man-made fabric known as 'Vetbed'. The mother can escape from its heat by lying at the side of the pad. The use of this type of bedding gives the babies an opportunity to get a purchase on the surface with their needle claws when they push against the teats to feed, thus developing their leg muscles.

## SUCCESSFUL MATING

There are variations in terms of which day is right, and if the bitch will not accept the dog the chances are that it is too early. Most stud owners will keep the bitch for a day or two, trying each day until they achieve success. A successful mating does not necessarily mean that the bitch conceives; infertility in both dogs and bitches is not unknown, and after a failure for any reason, veterinary help should be sought and tests made of both male and female dogs.

## DIET AND EXERCISE DURING PREGNANCY

■ For the first four weeks, normal routine will apply and you should continue feeding high-quality food, not forgetting one capsule of cod liver oil daily. Do not take the advice of anyone other than expert breeders or the vet; over-feeding and over-supplementation can have disastrous effects.

■ Perhaps a little more care than usual is necessary to prevent the bitch from jumping and falling, but exercise should be taken regularly.

■ At four weeks plus, the bitch should have more food than usual, but bear in mind that as she becomes distended her stomach will be less capable of taking the food, and therefore her meals should be divided into two parts.

■ Consideration can be given to an increase in vitamins and certain minerals, but care should be taken not to exceed the amounts quoted. Consult your vet if in doubt.

■ Milk and eggs can be added to the bitch's diet with the addition of a teaspoon of corn or olive oil, and her motions should be regular and firm.

■ I have always included a raspberry leaf tablet during the last week, as I have found that this facilitates the birth process. At this stage, the food intake may be increased by up to twenty-five per cent, given in four or five portions during the day.

## PREPARATION FOR WHELPING

Not a lot of equipment is necessary for whelping but when the time comes, the following list is for guidance only:

- Newspapers
- Surgical scissors
- 30 cm (12 in) squares of clean old towelling
- Gentle veterinary antiseptic
- A plastic rubbish bag.
- Whelping box and heat pad.

- A can of puppy milk replacer
- Little animal feed bottles and teats
- A book describing the birth process by a practising breeder

When you're ready with everything assembled, give instructions to the family to keep away, and then phone your vet and tell him when you are expecting. Hopefully, you will not need his expertise but be prepared. Remember to phone him when the whelping starts.

## The birth

There are no absolute norms, and there's something slightly different with every birth. For instance, usually the bitch's temperature will drop from 38.5°C (101.4°F), which is the average dog's temperature, down to anything between 36.1-37.2°C (97-99°F) about twenty-four hours prior to the birth. However, this is not always the case and sometimes it's only twelve hours before, so don't rely on it happening according to the book. She may refuse food twelve hours prior to giving birth; she may not.

- For the sake of hygiene and ease of birth, trim away the hair from the vulva and anus area and away from the teats so that the new-born pups have easy access to their milk.
- Some bitches appear very anxious, panting continually and scratching up the bedding or newspaper as their time approaches. Your dog may do this for twenty-four hours or she may be calm until she starts her labour.

- By now she should be familiar with her whelping box and she should be watched for signs of the first contractions.
- There is a school of thought that the bitch should be left to her own devices: that she'll know what to do by nature. The other school believes that we have removed dogs so far from their natural behaviour that it behoves us to assist as much as we can. The middle ground is probably the best, so observe the bitch and offer help and encouragement as necessary. Family dogs like to be close to their owners at times of stress.
- Sometimes maiden bitches are scared of their own puppies and with the first one or two, they haven't a clue what to do and need encouragement, whereas others know by a powerful instinct.

# WHELPING

1 Scrub your hands and nails and wait. The first visible contractions are weak and come with a fairly long interval in between them, gradually getting closer and stronger until you can see the strain. The first sign of impending birth is usually a grey membrane, looking like a balloon, protruding from the vulva. It contains a green fluid and can come and go many times before anything happens. Don't break this membrane, but when it is at its biggest, check it with a gentle squeeze. If it is hard, then it is the puppy bag and the other bag has probably burst of its own accord.

2 When a puppy is actually born, break the membranes with your nails carefully. The puppy will still be attached to its umbilical cord. About 5 cm (2 in) from the puppy, squeeze the umbilical cord between finger and thumb and cut the cord.

3 The bitch may expel the after-birth (placenta) and you should dispose of this in a plastic bag. It is possible that the bitch may get to the placenta before you do, but don't worry as it is perfectly natural for her to eat it, the theory being that it contains essential minerals and vitamins. She will also want to clear it before any predators get wind of it.

4 Hold the puppy gently in a square of the prepared towelling, and clear any mucus in the nose or mouth. You may have to open the mouth to do this so be gentle bearing in mind that the bones are not ossified and can be easily damaged.

5 Hold the puppy upside down and vigorously dry it with the towelling; it should open its mouth and squeak. A first-time mother can sometimes get a panic attack and be quite harsh with the new-born puppy because she doesn't know what to do. Keep her calm and don't let her do anything you might regret.

## INERTIA

This is when the bitch will either not start her contractions or she does start but nothing happens and they become progressively weaker until the bitch is exhausted. The first type is known as primary inertia and the other is secondary inertia. Should you diagnose either condition, a vet should be called immediately to administer a pituitary injection which should start her labour again within a short space of time. If the treatment fails, a Caesarean section will be performed.

Do not be over-anxious; the tendency with today's vets is to get into Caesarean sections rather too quickly. Skilled breeders usually wait about two hours before summoning veterinary help.

6 During this time the bitch will be anxiously licking her newly arrived puppy, and the experience will stimulate her milk. Put the puppy on a teat; the two rear teats are richer in colostrum which is the substance containing antibodies to counter the main diseases. You may have to express a drop of milk from the nipple, open the puppy's jaws and place them round the nipple, teaching it how to suck. This is particularly the case when the puppies are born early, as often they don't seem to be programmed fully.

7 The remaining puppies should follow in the course of the next few hours; the time lapse also varies with each litter.

8 In the breaks between deliveries, offer the bitch some glucose water or honey-sweetened milk to replenish her energy. It is not always easy to tell when all the puppies have been born and sometimes your dog may surprise you and produce a live one hours after the main event. Keep an eye on her for any contractions and count the number of afterbirths – there should be an equal number of placentas and puppies.

9 When she settles down and sleeps with her young contentedly suckling, she has probably finished. Later the vet can give the bitch an injection to clear any debris which is left inside her and thereby help prevent infection.

10 After your bitch has finished whelping, you should take her outside to relieve herself. She may be unwilling to leave her offspring but she must go. Her motions may be loose but this is probably due to the placentas that she may have eaten, and at this juncture it is of no great consequence and you should not worry.

11 Take this opportunity to clear the whelping box of any soiled paper and replace it with the 'vetbed'. During the next eight hours, you should clean the mother using a mild disinfectant and make sure that the residue is washed off so that the puppies cannot ingest it.

## BREECH BIRTH

If there appears to be an obstruction and part of the puppy has emerged and stops, as sometimes happens with a breech birth, there is no alternative but to pull the puppy out. Hold it lightly in the towelling and gently pull in time with the contractions. When the bitch stops contracting you should stop pulling. Take it easy because the puppy is delicate.

# POST-NATAL CARE

The bitch will now become a milk-producing machine. She will require three to four times the usual amount of food with plenty of water and milk.

## Eclampsia

Because of the enormous demands made on her system she may have trouble in producing enough calcium for the puppies, and may suffer from a condition known as eclampsia. This is serious: she may puff a lot, appearing distressed around her puppies. She may be restless, and if she staggers when she walks immediate and emergency veterinary attention is required. The vet will inject her with calcium boroglucinate and, almost like magic, the condition will disappear. If vetinerary assistance is not sought, the bitch may die. It is of some help to supplement the food with calcium and vitamin D two weeks before the birth but take advice.

## Mastitis

This is another condition to which nursing mothers are prone. It is an infection of the milk-producing glands and shows itself as a reddening around the teats and a hardening of the breast. It will need the vet's attention, but in the meantime bathe the whole area in warm water and gently express some milk, removing the pressure, and put a puppy onto the teat.

## Development of the puppies

■ On the second or third day, the puppies' dew claws are removed. If the breeder has no experience, it is better that the vet attends to this minor operation. At the same time, the tail can be docked. There is some controversy about tail docking, and the law in the UK states that only vets can perform this simple operation but some of them may refuse. However, there is no reason why

### MONITORING THE PUPPIES' PROGRESS

The one sure way to monitor the progress of puppies is to weigh them on a daily basis and carefully record the result. They should double their birth weight in the first two weeks. They must be monitored carefully if they fail to have a small weight increase daily. There may be various reasons for this: the mother's milk may be in short supply or not palatable, she may not allow them to feed, or their claws may be too sharp. If you cannot find the reason, it will be necessary to supplement the puppies' food with milk replacer.

undocked puppies should not be shown.

■ Between ten and fourteen days, the puppies' eyes will open. Up until this time, there is little to do except to keep their quarters clean and ensure a regular supply of food and water. As her family gets older, the bitch may want to leave them for short periods of time, so be certain to allow her to do this.

■ When the pups' eyes and ears open everything changes; almost overnight the puppies will become more active and exploratory. After a few days they will be quite strong on their legs and it will be time to let them out of the whelping box. A pen made up of wire panels used for composting garden waste makes an ideal

***It is a good idea to ask your vet to examine the young puppies.***

play pen. Cover the floor with sheets of newspaper. It has the advantage of being the start of house-training; the puppies will wander out of their sleeping quarters to defecate and urinate, as they do not like to foul their own nest.

## Weaning

The weaning process starts from when the puppies are about three weeks old. The bitch will indicate that she wants to get away from her brood, and this is an ideal time to introduce the puppies to new foods. Perhaps the easiest way is to scrape a piece of raw braising steak into a paste with a sharp knife and let the puppies lick it off your fingertips. In a short time, they'll get accustomed to this and will take it off a plate. It will lead naturally to feeding them small quantities of scrambled egg with milk replacer and thence to a regular puppy food in cans or a complete diet made moist.

Let the puppies suckle the mother but at the same time begin to reduce her food intake. Her milk supply will gradually dry up and the suckling is more for comfort than for food. It is not necessary to remove the bitch from her youngsters altogether; they wean themselves naturally following this system. Cow's milk is not suitable for puppies; it does not have the required nutrient value nor is it digestible enough. Buy a good-quality milk replacer which is specially formulated for puppies from the vet. Within ten days you should be feeding the puppies six times a day with small amounts.

Typical feeding should be at four-hourly intervals, starting at 8am and finishing at 10pm.

- The first meal of the day would be moist complete puppy food.
- The second: crushed boiled egg or scrambled egg.
- The third: minced beef, either raw or lightly cooked, or chicken.
- The fourth: crushed boiled egg or scrambled egg.
- The fifth: raw or lightly cooked minced beef, or chicken.
- Lastly: a dish of warm milk.

The mother will gradually become less interested in feeding the pups, and the first indications are that she will stand, making it difficult for them to reach her. She will also object to the pin-prick nails of the puppies as they massage her teats. The extreme tips of these nails can be cut carefully with scissors to stop them scratching the bitch.

## Vaccination and worming

Nowadays a vaccine against parvovirus can be administered from about six weeks onwards; this is a wise precaution. Puppy wormers are available and should be given to the litter at about three weeks and again at five and seven weeks.

### FINDING THE RIGHT BUYER

Finally, enlist the help of your bitch's breeder to select the best puppy to keep for breeding or exhibition. Be careful to find suitable homes for those you cannot keep. You will have gone to considerable trouble to produce good puppies, and it behoves you to find good homes for them. Supply the new owners with:

- A week's supply of food
- A diet sheet
- Kennel Club papers
- A month's insurance
- A promise to help in the future if needs be

The mother should be wormed at the same time because the likelihood will be that she will reinfest herself from her own puppies when she cleans them.

## Socialization

For the first three weeks, there should be no visitors outside the immediate family because the mother can become stressed and there is a risk of infection. Children should not be allowed to handle the puppies until they get bigger and stronger, and then they should be handled with care.

Socialization is of the utmost importance, and the puppies should be subjected to as many experiences as possible, including gentle grooming.

# 6

# SHOWING YOUR DOG

## HISTORY AND RINGCRAFT

Competition between dog owners to select the best working dog began in England around 1775 when people started showing Fox Hounds, and progressed through early agricultural shows with working sheep dogs to the cities where urban man, following his agricultural inclinations, used his dogs for 'sport', e.g. killing rats in the pits of London pubs. Dog shows, as we know them, began in pubs in the mid-1800s, where men would meet to gamble on the expertise of their terriers and afterwards discuss and match their dogs. From these humble beginnings, privately organised beauty shows sprang up. They were staged originally as profitable commercial enterprises, and the chief entrepreneur in this field was Charles Cruft who made a good living from dogs. He was quick to perceive the changes in the economic and social structure of nineteenth-century Britain: increased leisure time and more money coupled with the growth of the middle classes.

### Early dog shows

These early shows were not the well-run functions we see today. Any rules that existed were ignored, and competitors resorted to every conceivable bit of skulduggery because winning dogs commanded very high prices. As the aristocracy was getting interested, such scandalous behaviour was deplored.

### The Kennel Club

This gentleman's club, which was founded in 1873, devised a set of simple rules to control the criminal element at their own events and enhance the public perception of dog shows, thus improving their own finances. They succeeded in their aims, and other show organisers, recognising the benefits, applied to the Kennel Club for permission to impose the same rules. By granting permission, the Kennel Club virtually took over the government of shows throughout Great Britain. When Queen Victoria's dogs were shown, the future of showing was guaranteed and incidentally set the

*Traditionally, Yorkshire Terriers are the only breed shown on fabric-covered boxes. This stems from when they were shown without leads.*

pattern for women's involvement, which has developed to such an extent that women now dominate showing and breeding dogs.

Today, the vast majority of dog shows are licensed by the Kennel Club and dogs must be registered with them before they can be entered. Showing registered dogs at unlicensed shows is frowned upon severely and can lead to disciplinary action.

## Ringcraft

Phone the Kennel Club for details of ringcraft clubs in your area; they are the focal point for the exhibitor. Experienced people teach the skills required in showing all breeds for exhibition, and some will

### WARNING

Dog showing can be seriously addictive! It is a fact that many people become so obsessed with exhibiting their dogs that they change their life-style, some to the extent of changing their career or even moving house in the search for more room and privacy to breed dogs. There is a sub-culture centred around pedigree dogs, which is controlled by the Kennel Club. It has strictly enforced rules to which breeders and exhibitors are expected to adhere. By careful application, ordinary people can become authorities of their chosen breed.

include obedience and agility. They usually meet once a week and, for a small fee, anyone can enjoy a pleasant evening in convivial company learning the basics of an absorbing hobby.

## Ring etiquette

This will also be taught, and it is very important as there are things you should not do when showing your dog:

■ Never engage the judge in conversation – just answer his or her questions.

■ Nobody should allow their dog to interfere with or even disturb another.

■ Never argue with a decision – just accept it with grace even if you disagree. There will be another show and another judge – today's placings may be reversed tomorrow, such is the nature of dog showing.

## The art of ringcraft

Not only will you learn the technicalities of ringcraft but also you will teach your dog to enjoy showing.

■ Teach him to stand still for the examination and how to walk; if the judge cannot see the movement properly he is unlikely to place your dog. It is not simply a question of putting a dog on the lead and walking round – a Yorkshire Terrier should walk happily, head held proudly with the ears up giving the impression of vivacity. Some dogs show

*This line of show dogs is having a last-minute grooming before judging.*

naturally on the show box, whereas others require some gentle persuasion.

■ You have to learn the various patterns that judges may ask you to walk; these may be a straight line, a triangle or a circle. Judges do this in order to view the dog from all angles. They have only a couple of minutes in which to assess the dog so it is up to you to present him in the best possible light.

■ Go to as many shows as possible to study ringwork and grooming for show dogs. Your friendly breeder will help, provided that your questions are asked after, and not before or during, showing. Many competitors are in a state of nerves until they have finished. The ease with

which the professional handler shows a dog is deceiving and comes from years of practice. He knows how to emphasise his dog's good points and how to minimize his bad ones, not only in the ring but also in the trimming.

## Record keeping

Puppies are shown at between six and twelve months of age. Great care must be taken with the keeping of records because the class in which a dog can be entered is governed by his previous wins and possibly age. The class definitions appear in the schedules and if a dog is entered in a class for which he is not eligible, he will be disqualified and his winnings removed. It is also important that no mistakes are made on the entry form for the same reason.

## SHOW PRESENTATION

Presentation, grooming and condition are of ultimate importance. No judge is going to consider an out-of-condition, miserable dog with a scruffy, unkempt coat. Conditioning a dog means not only exercising and feeding him properly but also developing his mind.

### The show coat

The two most important steps for maintaining a show coat on a Yorkie are oiling and putting it in paper crackers.

*This Yorkie is in paper crackers to keep his show coat straight and in first-class condition.*

- The oil used depends on the type of coat. A light dressing of oil should be applied every day to soften the hair and prevent splits, and the dog should be bathed every two or three weeks or the valuable hair may come out in the comb.
- The dog must be trained to accept the crackers on the various parts of the body. The topknot is usually the first, and when the hair is long enough a cracker is put in with care so as not to pull the skin. He is likely to scratch it off and it may be necessary to replace it many times over for a few days until he ignores it.
- Next, the mouth hair is crackered so it does not interfere with the mouth opening or hitting the eyes when he is running about. When he is used to it, a small one is put in the beard.
- The dog must be accustomed gently to crackering all over and oiling as it will have to be done every day. Up to twenty-six crackers will be needed and considerable care must be exercised when doing it because mistakes will cause loss and deterioration in the length and quality of the coat.

### Bathing and blow-drying

You must also learn the art of bathing the dog and blow-drying without causing crinkles or waves. Again, this will be new to a puppy and will require patient training.

■ At this point it should be noted that the moustaches are better trimmed when wet.

■ The hair should always be brushed downwards and then parted, and the same action is repeated over the entire body.

■ The air must not be too hot or it will burn the delicate hair and dry the skin. Neither must it stay on one spot for long.

■ About two weeks before the show, wash and dry your dog. Give him a centre parting from head to tail, and stand him on a table with one side hanging over the edge.

■ Trim from front to back with very

## TOOLS

Buy the best equipment available, taking advice from established exhibitors. The following list may be helpful:

■ Pair of high-quality hairdresser's scissors

■ Steel comb with both close- and wide-set teeth

■ Almond oil, a saucer and pure-bristle brush

■ Strips of acid-free tissue paper, 17 cm (7 in) long and 7 cm (2 1/2 in) wide

■ Small elastic bands to hold crackers (wrappings)

■ Nail clippers

■ Cotton wool for cleaning the eyes and ears

■ A baby's toothbrush and doggy toothpaste

*Showing should be fun and enjoyable for you and your Yorkie, even though you will both need patience.*

sharp scissors so that the length just reaches the surface.

■ With the dog facing away from you, comb the back hair over the table and trim across it, starting and finishing with a curve. Trim the beard in the same way.

■ Trim away any loose ends. The hair on the legs is combed to the table top and trimmed just above the surface, and the chest hair is also combed to the table and then cut level.

## SHOWING AND JUDGING

There are several different types of show, details of which can be obtained from the Kennel Club in the UK. They accommodate dogs at different levels of winning.

■ **Knock-out Matches** are the lowest level of competition and are held by the training clubs. Entry fees are very low and entries are made on the night. Two dogs are drawn and matched against each other, the winner going on to the next round with gradual elimination until only one is left.

■ **Exemption Shows,** also at the lower end of the scale, are fun shows held at minor agricultural shows, garden fêtes and the like. Entries are cheap and taken on the field at the show. There are usually four pedigree classes and many fun classes for the family.

■ **Sanction and Limited Shows** have limitations placed on them as to who can enter. Both can be entered and the fees paid prior to the show, and the closing dates and limits are advertised.

■ **Primary Shows** are comparatively new, and entries on the night are open to everyone. As in the previous shows,

*Winning makes all the hard work worthwhile. Even the dog enjoys his moment of success.*

the dog must have won nothing towards his championship.

■ **Open Shows** are very popular and are open to all dogs regardless of winnings. Entries are made before the show and the closing day must be adhered to.

### Championship shows

To become a champion a dog must win three Challenge Certificates under three different judges, one of which must be

won after the dog is twelve months old. The Certificates, also known as 'tickets' or CC's, can be won at the specified Championship Shows only. There are three categories of Championship Shows:

- The Breed Club Shows.
- The Group Shows (breeds are divided into six groups: Terrier, Toy, Hound, Gundog, Working and Utility).
- The General Championship Shows, which must be entered several weeks in advance and the fees paid. They are the most expensive to enter.
- For the 'Junior Warrant', dogs compete for points and when twenty- five are won, you are entitled to claim the warrant from the Kennel Club. There are three points for a win in breed classes at Championship Shows when Challenge Certificates are on offer, and one point for a win where they are not on offer or at an Open Show. The dogs can only compete between the ages of twelve and eighteen months.

## Judging

To become a judge you have to satisfy yourself that you have an in-depth knowledge of your own dog and your breed. The process of learning starts the moment you become involved. Having the desire to learn, you will read, attend seminars and take courses such as the Judges Diploma Course. You will steward at all levels and be seen enthusiastically taking part in canine events and probably start your apprenticeship by judging Club Matches and Exemption Shows.

## Juniors

In the UK, two organisations cater for young persons between the ages of eight and eighteen: the Kennel Club Junior Organisation (KCJO), which is run on a regional basis, and the Junior Handlers Association (JHA), organised on a national basis. The KCJO exists to further the knowledge and understanding of pedigree dogs in young people via education and competition, especially the International Junior Handler of the Year, which is the world's most prestigious junior competition and takes place annually at Crufts. The JHA organises a competition through the Open Shows on a country-wide basis in the UK and culminating in the title of Junior Handler of the Year.

## Successful showing

Buying a Yorkshire Terrier may lead you into realms about which you have never dreamt. Great careers have been built on the breeding and exhibition of dogs, but it requires hard work and total dedication to the breed. With all animals, there will be sadness and disappointments but the moments of triumph and the hours of pleasure will far outweigh anything you have ever experienced, if you've got what it takes.

# PART THREE

# HEALTHCARE

In this section on healthcare, there is expert practical advice on how to keep your dog fit and healthy and prevent many common health problems, together with information on feeding, exercise, care of the older dog, common canine illnesses and diseases and the special health problems that may affect the Yorkshire Terrier as a breed, especially inherited ones. Essential first-aid techniques for use in a wide range of common accidents and emergencies, including road accidents and dog fights, are also featured, with easy-to-follow step-by-step illustration guides where applicable, and advice on when you should seek expert veterinary help.

# CHAPTER SEVEN

# HEALTH MAINTENANCE

Throughout the health section of this book, where comments relate equally to the dog or the bitch, we have used the term 'he' to avoid the repeated, clumsy use of 'he or she'. Your Yorkshire Terrier is definitely not an 'it'.

## SIGNS OF A HEALTHY DOG

### ■ General appearance

In general, a healthy dog looks healthy. He wants to play with you, as games are a very important part of a dog's life. A Yorkshire Terrier, although a tiny dog in the physical sense, thinks big and is a very energetic dog and always ready for his walk.

### ■ Eyes

His dark eyes are bright and alert and, apart from the small amount of 'sleep' in the inner corners, there is no discharge. His nose is usually cold and wet with no discharge, although a little clear fluid can be normal.

### ■ Ears

His ears are also alert and very responsive to sounds around him. The Yorkshire Terrier's ears are carried erect and have a covering of short hair. The inside of his ear flap is pale pink or grey in appearance and silky in texture. No wax will be visible and there will be no unpleasant smell. He will not scratch his ears much, or shake his head excessively.

### ■ Coat

A healthy Yorkshire Terrier's coat will be quite long, straight, glossy and feel pleasant and silky to the touch. The dog will not scratch excessively and scurf will be not be present. His coat will smell 'doggy' but not unpleasant, and he will probably continuously shed hairs (moult) to some degree, especially if he lives indoors with the family.

### ■ Tail

A Yorkshire Terrier's tail, if left undocked at the natural length as many are nowadays, will taper gradually to the tip and be well covered in hair, especially at the base. If docked, as has been the custom, this will be to medium length. In law this can only be performed by a vet now.

### ■ Teeth

The teeth of a healthy dog should be white and smooth. If they are yellow and dull there may be plaque or tartar formation. All the temporary (milk) teeth should have been replaced by six months of age but the Yorkie seems to retain these more frequently than other breeds. If present they will need veterinary attention (see Health Maintenance, page 103, and also Special Problems of the Yorkshire Terrier, page 105).

### ■ Claws and feet

A Yorkie's claws, which are black, should not be broken or too long. There is a short non-sensitive tip, as in our nails. The claw should end at the ground, level with the pad. Dogs will not pay much attention to their feet, apart from normal washing, but excessive licking can indicate disease. Yorkshire Terriers are usually born with five toes on the front feet,

## POINTS OF THE YORKSHIRE TERRIER

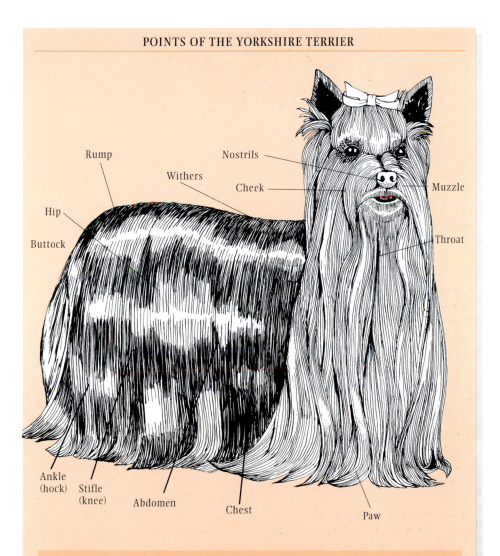

The major points of the dog are shown on the illustration above. Some of the terminology used is the same as that of the human body, but some terms may be unfamiliar, e.g. stifles (for knees) and hocks (for ankles). For an even more detailed breakdown of the parts of the dog, turn to the glossary (see page 137).

## EXAMINING YOUR DOG

- The ears should not smell unpleasant, and there should be no visible wax.

- Check the dog's eyes and nose. There should be no discharges.

- The dog should not be too fat nor too thin. He should look healthy and in good condition.

- The coat should be glossy and pleasant to touch. There should be no scurf.

- The teeth should be white and smooth, with no plaque or tartar.

- The claws should not be broken nor too long. They should end level with the pad.

with one in our 'thumb' position called the dew claw, and four on the hind feet. If a puppy is born with a dew claw on a hind foot, it is usually removed at three to five days of age as they become pendulous and are often injured as an adult.

- **Stools**

A healthy dog will pass stools between once and six times a day depending on diet, temperament, breed and opportunity.

- **Urination**

A male dog will urinate numerous times on a walk as this is territorial behaviour. Bitches usually urinate less often.

- **Weight**

A healthy dog will look in good bodily condition for his size – not too fat and not too thin. Sixty per cent of dogs nowadays are overweight, so balance the diet with the right amount of exercise.

- **Feeding**

A dog will usually be ready for his meal and, once adult, he should be fed regularly at the same time each day. Most dogs require one meal a day, but some healthy dogs seem to require two meals daily just to maintain a normal weight. These are the very active dogs who tend to 'burn off' more calories.

## CARE OF THE OLDER DOG

Provided that he has been well cared for throughout his life, there will be no need to treat the older Yorkshire Terrier any differently as old age approaches. Yorkshire Terriers usually live longer than most larger breeds, and we have seen many a Yorkshire Terrier of fourteen or more. However, twelve years is a reasonable average life expectancy for this breed.

■ **Diet**

This should be chosen to:

■ Improve existing problems

■ Slow or prevent the development of disease

■ Enable the dog to maintain his ideal body weight

■ Be highly palatable and digestible

■ Contain an increased amount of fatty acids, vitamins (especially A, B and E) and certain minerals, notably zinc

■ Contain reduced amounts of protein, phosphorus and sodium

■ **Fitness and exercise**

A healthy Yorkshire Terrier should hardly need to reduce his exercise until he is ten to twelve years old. There should be no sudden change in routine; a sudden increase in exercise is as wrong as a sudden drop. Let the dog tell you when he has had enough. If he lags behind, has difficulty in walking, breathing, or getting to his feet after a long walk, then it is time to consider a health check. As dogs age, they need a good diet, company, comfort, and a change of scenery to add interest to their lives.

■ **Avoiding obesity**

As the body ages, all body systems age with it. The heart and circulation, lungs, muscles and joints are not as efficient. These should all be able to support and transport a dog of the correct weight but may fail if the dog is grossly overweight.

A dog of normal weight will approach old age with a greater likelihood of reaching it. It is wise to diet your dog at this stage if you have let his weight increase. Food intake can be increased almost to normal when the weight loss has been achieved.

■ Reduce the calorie intake to about sixty per cent of normal, to encourage the conversion of body fat back into energy.

■ Feed a high-fibre diet so that the dog does not feel hungry.

■ Provide maintenance levels of essential nutrients, such as protein, vitamins and minerals, so that deficiencies do not occur.

**Note:** your veterinary surgeon will be able to supply or advise on the choice of several prescription low-calorie diets, which are available in both dried and canned form, or will instruct you on how to mix your own.

**The dog's lifespan**

Most people assume that seven years of our lives are equivalent to one year of a dog's. However, a more accurate comparison would be as follows:

■ 1 dog year = 15 human years

■ 3 dog years = 30 human years

■ 6 dog years = 40 human years

■ 9 dog years = 55 human years

■ 12 dog years = 65 human years

■ 15 dog years = 80 human years

**Note:** This is only an approximate guide as the larger breeds of dog tend not to live as long as the smaller breeds.

## DIET

### For puppies

■ The correct diet as a pup is essential to allow him to achieve his full potential during the growing phase. In a Yorkshire Terrier this lasts up to fifteen months of age. Many home-made diets are deficient in various ingredients just because owners do not fully appreciate the balance that is required. It is far better to rely on one of the correctly formulated and prepared commercial diets, which will contain the correct amounts and proportions of essential nutrients such as protein, carbohydrates, fats, roughage, minerals, such as calcium and phosphorus, and essential vitamins.

■ Modern thinking is that the complete, dried, extruded diets available now have so many advantages that the new puppy could be put on to a 'growth' formula diet of this type from as early as four weeks. Crunchy diets such as these have advantages in dental care also.

■ However, there are some excellent canned

### DIET CHECKLIST

Here are some basic guidelines for feeding your dog.
■ Feed puppies a special puppy or growth-formula food until they are twelve to eighteen months old
■ Feed adult dogs an adult maintenance version
■ Feed older dogs, over ten to twelve years of age, a specially formulated diet
■ Ask your vet for advice on feeding your dog correctly

and semi-moist diets available but care should be taken to check whether these are complete diets, or complementary foods which require biscuits and other ingredients to be added. If you really know your diets, it is of course possible to formulate a home-prepared diet from fresh ingredients.

■ Your Yorkshire Terrier puppy should be fed four times a day until he is three months of age, and with a complete dried food this can be left down so that he can help himself to food whenever he feels hungry. The exact amount of food will depend on his age and the type of food, and if instructions are not included on the packet, you should consult your vet.

■ At three months of age, he should be fed three times daily, but each meal should have more food in it. By six months of age, he could be down to two larger meals a day, still of a puppy or growth-formula food. He should remain on this type of food until he is twelve to fifteen months of age, and then change to an adult maintenance version.

### Adult dogs

■ They can be fed on any one of the excellent range of quality dog foods now available. Your vet is the best person to advise you as to the best diet for your Yorkshire Terrier, and this advice will vary depending on his age, amount of exercise and condition.

■ From the age of ten to twelve years onwards, your Yorkshire Terrier may benefit from a change to a diet specially formulated for the older dog, as he will have differing requirements as his body organs age. Your vet is the best person with whom to discuss this as he will be able to assess your dog's general condition and requirements.

## VACCINATIONS

Vaccination is the administration of a modified live or killed form of an infection which does not cause illness in the dog, but instead stimulates the formation of antibodies against the disease itself.

- **Four major diseases**
- There are four major diseases against which all dogs should be vaccinated. These are as follows:
  - Canine distemper (also called hardpad)
  - Infectious canine hepatitis
  - Leptospirosis
  - Canine parvovirus

Many vaccination courses now include a component against parainfluenza virus, one of the causes of kennel cough, that scourge of boarding and breeding kennels. A separate vaccine against bordetella, another cause of kennel cough, can be given in droplet form down the nose prior to your dog entering boarding kennels. All these diseases are described in Chapter 8 (see page 107).

- **When to vaccinate**
- In the puppy, vaccination should start at eight to ten weeks of age, and is a course of two injections, two to four weeks apart.
- It is recommended that adult dogs have a check-up and booster vaccination by the vet every year.

## EXERCISE

### For puppies

- As a puppy, your Yorkshire Terrier should not be given too much exercise. At the age that you acquire him, usually at six to eight weeks old, he will need gentle, frequent forays into your garden, or other people's gardens provided they are not open to stray dogs. He can and should meet other vaccinated, reliable dogs or puppies and play with them. He will also enjoy energetic games with you, but remember that in any tug-of-war type of contest you should win.

- Although you should be taking him out with you to accustom him to the sights and sounds of normal life, at this stage you should not put him down on the ground in public places until the vaccination course is completed, because of the risk of infection.

Carrying a Yorkie puppy everywhere with you is simple compared with the larger breeds so you should maximize this opportunity to socialize him early.

- About a week after his second vaccination, you will be able to take him out for walks, but remember that at this stage he is equivalent to a toddler. His bones have not calcified, his joints are still developing, and too much strenuous exercise can affect normal development. Perhaps three walks daily for about half an hour each is ample by about four months of age, rising to two to three hours by the time he reaches six months. At this stage, as his bones and joints develop, he could then be taken for more vigorous runs in the country. However, he should not be involved in really tiring exercise until he is nine months to a year old, by which time his joints have almost fully matured, and his bones have fully calcified.

## Adult dogs

■ As an adult dog, his exercise tolerance will be almost limitless, certainly better than most of us. This is surprising in one so small, but it is essential that such a lively, active, intelligent breed as the Yorkshire Terrier has an adequate amount of exercise daily. A daily quota of at least an hour or so of interesting, energetic exercise is advisable.

### DAILY CARE

There are several things that you should be carrying out daily for your dog to keep him in first-class condition.

■ **Grooming**

All dogs benefit from a daily grooming. Use a stiff brush or comb obtained from your vet or pet shop, and ensure you specify that it is for a Yorkshire Terrier with a fine, silky coat, as brushes vary. Comb or brush in the direction of the lie of the hair. Hair is constantly growing and being shed, especially in dogs that live indoors with us, as their bodies become confused as to which season it is in a uniformly warm house. Brushing removes dead hair and scurf, and stimulates the sebaceous glands to produce the natural oils that keep the coat glossy.

■ **Bathing**

Yorkies should not require frequent baths, but can benefit from a periodic shampoo using a dog shampoo with a conditioner included.

■ **Feeding**

Dogs do not benefit from a frequently changed diet. Their digestive systems seem to get used to a regular diet; nor do they worry if they have the same food every day – that is a human trait – so establish a complete nutritious diet that your dog enjoys and stick to it. Yorkshire Terriers rarely have digestive problems but a regular established daily diet is one way of ensuring this.

The day's food should be given at a regular time each day. Usually the adult dog will have one meal a day, at either breakfast-time or teatime. Both are equally acceptable but ideally hard exercise should not be given within an hour of a full meal. It is better to

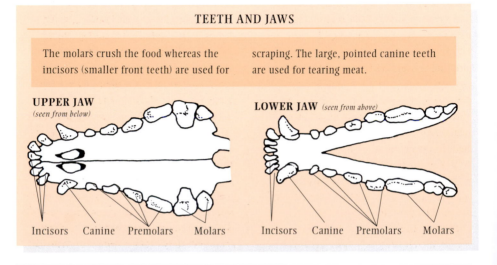

### TEETH AND JAWS

The molars crush the food whereas the incisors (smaller front teeth) are used for scraping. The large, pointed canine teeth are used for tearing meat.

**UPPER JAW** *(seen from below)*

Incisors   Canine   Premolars   Molars

**LOWER JAW** *(seen from above)*

Incisors   Canine   Premolars   Molars

give your dog a long walk and then feed him on your return. Some dogs seem to like two smaller meals a day, and this is perfectly acceptable, provided that the total amount of food given is not excessive.

■ **Water**

Your Yorkie should have a full bowl of clean, fresh water changed once or twice a day, and this should be permanently available. This is particularly important if he is on a complete dried food diet.

■ **Toileting**

Your dog should be let out into the garden first thing in the morning to toilet, and this can be taught quite easily on command and in a specified area of the garden. You should not take the dog out for a walk to toilet, unless you just do not have the space at home. The mess should be in your premises and then picked up and flushed down the toilet daily. Other people, children in particular, should not have to put up with our dogs' mess.

Throughout the day your dog should have access to a toileting area every few hours, and always last thing at night before you all retire to bed. Dogs will usually want to, and can be conditioned to, defecate immediately after a meal, so this should be encouraged.

■ **Company**

Yorkshire Terriers are very sociable dogs and require company, exercise and mental stimulation. There is no point having one unless you intend to be there most of the time. Obviously a well-trained and socialized adult should be capable of being left for one to three hours at a time, but puppies need constant attention if they are to grow up well balanced. Games, as mentioned before, are an essential daily pastime.

■ **Dental care**

Some complete diets are very crunchy.

## GENERAL INSPECTION

A full inspection of your dog is not necessary on a daily basis, unless you notice something different about him. However, it is as well to cast your eyes over him to ensure that:
■ The coat and skin are in good order
■ The eyes are bright
■ The ears are clean
■ The dog is not lame
Check that he has eaten his food, and that his stools and urine look normal.

Mimicking the texture of a wild dog's (e.g. fox or wolf) diet of a whole rabbit (bones, fur etc.), for instance, will keep the teeth relatively free of plaque and tartar. However, a daily teeth inspection is sensible. Lift the lips and look at not just the front incisors and canine teeth, but also the back premolars and molars. They should be a healthy, shiny white like ours.

If not, or if he is on a soft, canned or fresh meat diet, daily brushing using a toothbrush and enzyme toothpaste is advisable. Hide chew sticks help to clean teeth, as do root vegetables, such as carrots, and many vets recommend a raw marrow bone. However, these can occasionally cause teeth to break. Various manufacturers have brought out tasty, chewy food items that benefit teeth, and your vet will be able to recommend a suitable one.

Pups are born with, or acquire shortly after birth, a full set of temporary teeth. These start to be shed at about sixteen weeks of age with the central incisors, and the transition from temporary to permanent teeth should be

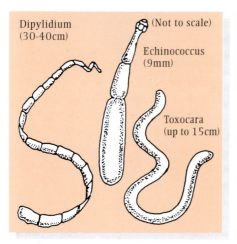

Dipylidium (30-40cm)
(Not to scale)
Echinococcus (9mm)
Toxocara (up to 15cm)

complete by six months of age. In the Yorkshire Terrier this mechanism seems to fail more often than other breeds so if extra teeth seem to be present, or if teeth seem out of position at this age, it is wise to seek your vet's advice (see Special Health Problems, page 105).

■ **General inspection**

A full inspection by you of your Yorkshire Terrier is not necessary on a daily basis, unless you notice something different about your dog. However, it is as well to cast your eyes over him to ensure that the coat and skin are in good order, his eyes are bright and his ears are clean, and he is not lame. Check that he has eaten his food, and that his stools and urine look normal.

## PERIODIC HEALTH CARE

### Worming

■ **Roundworms (Toxocara)**

All puppies should be wormed fortnightly from two weeks to three months of age, then monthly up to six months of age. Thereafter in a male or neutered female Yorkshire Terrier,

you should worm twice yearly. Dogs used for breeding have special roundworming requirements and you should consult your vet. There is evidence that entire females undergoing false (pseudo) pregnancies, have roundworm larvae migrating in their tissues, so they should be wormed at this time.

■ **Tapeworms (Dipylidium and Echinococcus)**

These need intermediate hosts (fleas and usually sheep offal respectively) to complete their life cycle, so prevention of contact with these is advisable. As a precaution, most vets recommend tapeworming adult dogs twice a year.

**Note:** There are very effective, safe combined round and tape wormers available now from your vet.

## SPECIAL HEALTH PROBLEMS

The Yorkshire Terrier is usually a fit, friendly and interesting companion. There are, however, some health problems that are known to occur in this breed particularly. A few of the commoner problems are detailed opposite.

### WORMING YOUR DOG

Dogs need to be wormed regularly for roundworms:

■ Fortnightly for puppies from two weeks to three months of age
■ Monthly for puppies from three months to six months of age
■ Twice yearly thereafter in male dogs and neutered females

**Note:** adult dogs should be wormed twice a year for tapeworms.

■ **Patella luxation**

This is an inherited problem in the Yorkshire Terrier. It is a dislocation of the patella (knee-cap) and is usually first apparent from about six months of age. The patella dislocates, usually to the inside of the leg, and can cause sudden lameness of the affected hind leg. Straightening the leg flicks the patella back into place and the dog can walk again for a while. If pain and lameness persist, surgery is necessary to replace the patella. Usually both stifles (knees) are affected.

■ **Perthe's Disease**

This is a disease affecting the development of one or both hip joints. It is seen especially in small terriers, and is hereditary in the Yorkshire Terrier. The bone of the head of the femur degenerates, producing severe pain and collapse of the joint. Failure of the blood supply to this small piece of bone is thought to be the cause.

■ **Tracheal collapse**

As the name suggests, this is the collapse and flattening of the windpipe between the dog's larynx and the chest. The cartilage rings that keep the trachea open to allow the easy passage of air become faulty and weak, and flatten. This narrows the trachea severely, and the dog can hardly breathe. Noisy, laboured breathing occurs, the dog is very weak and staggers, and death can occur. Surgery can be attempted but is usually unsuccessful.

■ **Milk teeth retention**

Retention of the temporary teeth beyond the age of six months seems to happen in the Yorkie more commonly than in other breeds. These milk teeth have long roots and if they

---

**NOTE**

In addition to the specific advice given here about special and inherited problems in the Yorkshire Terrier, you can reduce the chances of your new dog having these problems by asking the right questions about his ancestry before you purchase him. A good breeder will always be happy to discuss this with you.

---

are not shed they can adversely affect the eruption of the permanent teeth which may appear in the wrong place or in the wrong direction. This can affect the ability of the dog to open and close his mouth.

Sometimes the Yorkie seems to have a very overcrowded mouth with numerous temporary teeth which are retained into adulthood. This will lead to severe dental problems as food packs in between the dog's temporary and the permanent teeth. Periodontal disease (see Mouth problems, page 110) is not usually very long in following this dental problem.

**Treatment:** any temporary teeth that are retained after the age of six months should be extracted by the vet under a general anaesthetic.

■ **von Willebrand's Disease**

This is an inherited disease that is known to happen in the Yorkshire Terrier but is not at present a cause for alarm. It is a disease of a blood component, the platelets, and causes haemorrhage.

# CHAPTER EIGHT

# DISEASES AND ILLNESSES

■ **Rhinitis**

This infection of the nose is caused by viruses, bacteria or fungi, and is sometimes seen in the Yorkshire Terrier. It may also be part of a disease such as distemper or kennel cough. Sneezing or a clear or coloured discharge are the usual signs of rhinitis. Another cause, due to the dog's habit of sniffing, is a grass seed or other foreign object inhaled through the nostrils. The dog starts to sneeze violently, often after a walk through long grass.

■ **Tumours of the nose**

These are seen in the Yorkie. The first sign is often haemorrhage from one nostril. X-rays reveal a mass in the nasal chamber.

## Diseases producing a cough

A cough is a reflex that clears foreign matter from the bronchi, trachea and larynx. Severe inflammation of these structures will also stimulate the cough reflex.

■ **Laryngitis, tracheitis and bronchitis**

Inflammation of these structures can be caused by infection, such as kennel cough or

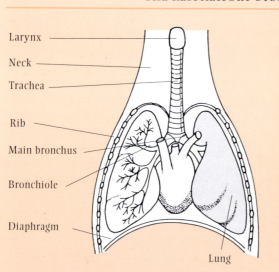

### THE RESPIRATORY SYSTEM

Larynx

Neck

Trachea

Rib

Main bronchus

Bronchiole

Diaphragm

Lung

The larynx, trachea, lungs and bronchi, together with the nose, make up the dog's respiratory system. Air is inhaled through the nose, filtered and passed through the larynx into the trachea. It enters the lungs through the bronchi, which subdivide into bronchioles and end in alveoli, or air sacs. Oxygen and carbon dioxide gases are exchanged in the alveoli.

## INFECTIOUS DISEASES

### ■ Distemper (hardpad)

This is a frequently fatal virus disease which usually affects dogs under one year of age. Affected dogs cough and have a discharge from the eyes and nose. Pneumonia often develops, and vomiting and diarrhoea usually follow. If the dog lives, nervous symptoms such as fits, paralysis or chorea (a type of regular twitch) are likely. The pads of the feet become thickened and hard – hence the other name for the disease, hardpad.

**Treatment:** antibiotics sometimes help, but the only real answer is prevention by vaccination as a puppy, and annual boosters thereafter.

### ■ Infectious canine hepatitis

This affects the liver. In severe cases, the first sign may be a dog completely off his food, very depressed and collapsed. Some die suddenly. Recovery is unlikely from this severe form of the disease. Prevention by vaccination is essential.

### ■ Leptospirosis

Two separate diseases affect dogs. Both, in addition to causing severe and often fatal disease in the dog, are infectious to humans.

■ Leptospira canicola causes acute kidney disease.

■ Leptospira icterohaemorrhagiae causes an acute infection of the liver, often leading to jaundice.

**Treatment:** this is often unsuccessful in both diseases, and prevention by vaccination is essential.

### ■ Canine parvovirus

This affects the bowels causing a sudden onset of vomiting and diarrhoea, often with blood, and severe depression. As death is usually due to dehydration, prompt replacement of the fluid and electrolyte loss is essential. In addition, antibiotics are also usually given to prevent secondary bacterial infection.

**Prevention:** this is by vaccination and is essential.

### ■ Kennel cough

This is a highly infectious cough occurring mainly in kennelled dogs. There are two main causes:

■ Bordetella, which is a bacterial infection.

■ Parainfluenza virus

Both of these affect the affected dog's trachea and lungs. Occasionally, a purulent discharge from the nose and eyes may develop. Antibiotics and rest are usually prescribed by the vet.

**Prevention:** both can be prevented by vaccination and this is recommended.

---

canine distemper, by irritant fumes or by foreign material. Usually, all three parts of the airway are affected at the same time.

Bronchitis is a major problem in the older dog caused by a persistent infection or irritation, producing irreversible changes in the bronchi. A cough develops and increases until the dog seems to cough almost constantly.

## Diseases producing laboured breathing

Laboured breathing is normally caused by those diseases that occupy space within the chest, and reduce the lung tissue available for oxygenation of the blood. An X-ray produces an accurate diagnosis.

■ **Tracheal collapse**

This is the collapse and flattening of the windpipe between the dog's larynx and the chest. The cartilage rings that keep the trachea open to allow the easy passage of air become faulty and weak, and flatten (see Special Problems of the Yorkshire Terrier, page 105).

■ **Pneumonia**

This is an infection of the lungs. Although it is relatively uncommon in the Yorkshire Terrier it does sometimes occur, and may be caused by viruses, bacteria, fungi or foreign material.

■ **Chest tumours**

These can cause respiratory problems by occupying lung space and by causing the accumulation of fluid within the chest.

## Accidents

Respiratory failure commonly follows accidents. Several types of injury may be seen:

■ **Haemorrhage into the lung** (Haemothorax) – rupture of a blood vessel in the lung will release blood which fills the air sacs.

■ **Free air in the chest** (Pneumothorax) – a ruptured lung allows air to surround the lungs and cause severe respiratory problems.

■ **Ruptured diaphragm** – this allows abdominal organs, such as the liver, spleen or stomach, to move forwards into the chest cavity.

### HEART AND CIRCULATION DISEASES

Heart attack in the human sense is uncommon. Collapse or fainting, however, does occur in Yorkies due to inadequate cardiac function, and tracheal collapse (see First Aid, page 131).

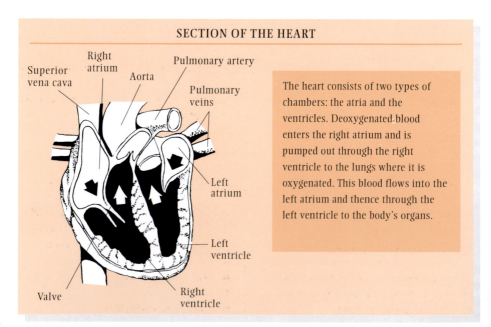

**SECTION OF THE HEART**

Superior vena cava

Right atrium

Aorta

Pulmonary artery

Pulmonary veins

Left atrium

Left ventricle

Right ventricle

Valve

The heart consists of two types of chambers: the atria and the ventricles. Deoxygenated blood enters the right atrium and is pumped out through the right ventricle to the lungs where it is oxygenated. This blood flows into the left atrium and thence through the left ventricle to the body's organs.

## THE CIRCULATORY SYSTEM

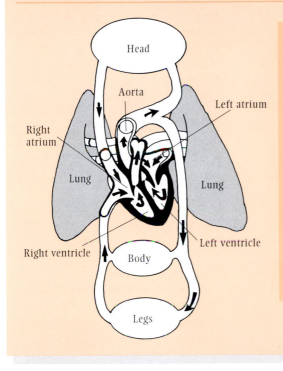

Head

Aorta

Left atrium

Right atrium

Lung

Lung

Right ventricle

Left ventricle

Body

Legs

Blood circulates around the dog's body by way of the circulatory system.

■ Oxygenated blood is pumped by the heart through the arteries to all the body organs, e.g. the brain, muscles and liver.

■ Oxygen and nutrients are extracted from the blood.

■ The used blood is returned by the veins to the right ventricle and then to the lungs.

■ In the lungs, carbon dioxide is exchanged for oxygen.

# Heart murmurs

■ **Acquired disease**

This may result from wear and tear or from inflammation of heart valves, problems of rhythm and rate, or disease of the heart muscle.

- ■ Weakness
- ■ Lethargy
- ■ Panting
- ■ Coughing
- ■ Abdominal distension
- ■ Collapse
- ■ Weight loss

# Congenital heart disease

This is usually due to valve defects or a hole in the heart. Signs of disease may include:

■ The sudden death of a pup

■ Weakness and failure to thrive or grow at a normal rate

**Note:** congestive heart failure is the end result of any of these defects.

# Heart block

Heart block is an acquired problem. A nerve impulse conduction failure occurs in the specialized heart muscle which is responsible for maintaining normal rhythm and rate. Signs of heart failure may include one or more of the following:

■ Exercise intolerance

■ Lethargy

■ Panting and/or coughing

- Enlargement of the abdomen due to fluid accumulation
- Poor digestion and weight loss

Veterinary investigation involves thorough examination, possibly X-rays of the chest, ECG, and, in some cases, ultrasound scanning.

## Blood clotting defects

Clotting problems may result from poisoning with Warfarin rat poison, not uncommon in an efficient rat-catching breed like a Yorkie. Haemorrhage then occurs which requires immediate treatment (see First Aid, page 129).

- **Congenital clotting defects** arise if the pup is born with abnormal blood platelets or clotting factors, both of which are essential in normal clotting. von Willebrand's disease is an inherited platelet disorder found occasionally.

## Tumours

The spleen, which is a reservoir for blood, is a relatively common site for tumours, especially in older dogs. Splenic tumours can bleed slowly into the abdomen or rupture suddenly, causing collapse. Surgical removal of the spleen is necessary.

### DIGESTIVE SYSTEM DISEASES

## Mouth problems

### Dental disease
- **Dental tartar**

This forms on the tooth surfaces when left-over food (plaque) solidifies on the teeth. This irritates the adjacent gum, causing pain, mouth odour, gum recession and, ultimately, tooth loss. This inevitable progression to periodontal disease may be prevented if plaque is removed by regular tooth brushing coupled with good diet, large chews and hard biscuits. Yorkies seem to be particularly prone to dental disease.

- **Periodontal disease** is inflammation and erosion of the gums around the tooth roots. Careful scaling and polishing of the teeth by your vet under an anaesthetic are necessary to save the teeth.
- **Dental caries** (tooth decay) is common in people, but not so in dogs *unless they are given chocolate and other sweet foods.*
- **Tooth fractures** can result from trauma in road accidents or if your Yorkshire Terrier is an enthusiastic stone chewer.
- **Retention of the temporary teeth** beyond the age of six months seems to happen in the Yorkie more commonly than in other breeds (see Health Maintenance, page 103, and Special Problems of the Yorkshire Terrier, page 105).

## Salivary cysts

These may occur as swellings under the tongue or neck, resulting from a ruptured salivary duct.

## Mouth tumours

These are often highly malignant, growing rapidly and spreading to other organs. First symptoms may be bad breath, increased salivation and bleeding from the mouth plus difficulties in eating.

## Foreign bodies in the mouth

(See First Aid, page 134).

## THE DIGESTIVE SYSTEM

The mouth, throat, oesophagus, stomach, intestines, liver and pancreas together make up the digestive system. When food is swallowed, it passes through the oesophagus into the stomach and intestines where it is broken down by enzymes. Nutrients are absorbed by the body, and waste matter is eliminated via the rectum.

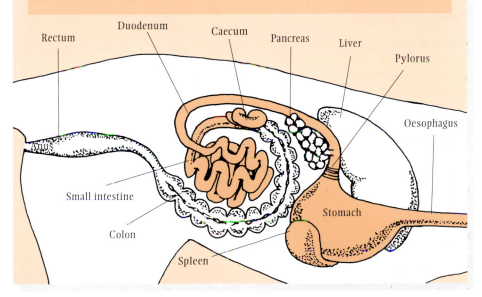

Duodenum · Rectum · Caecum · Pancreas · Liver · Pylorus · Oesophagus · Anus · Small intestine · Colon · Spleen · Stomach

## Problems causing vomiting

■ **Gastritis**

This is inflammation of the stomach and can result from unsuitable diet, scavenging or infection. The dog repeatedly vomits either food or yellowish fluid and froth, which may be blood stained.

■ **Obstruction of the oesophagus**

This condition leads to regurgitation of food immediately after feeding, and may be caused by small bones or other foreign bodies. Diagnosis is confirmed either by X-ray or by examination with an endoscope, and treatment must not be delayed.

■ **Obstruction lower down the gut, in the stomach or the intestine**

This may result from items such as stones, corks etc. Tumours can also lead to obstructive vomiting. The dog rapidly becomes very ill and the diagnosis is usually confirmed by palpation, X-rays or exploratory surgery.

■ **Intussusception**

This is telescoping of the bowel which can follow diarrhoea, especially in puppies. Surgery is essential.

## Pancreatic diseases

■ **Acute pancreatitis**

This is an extremely painful and serious

## PROBLEMS CAUSING DIARRHOEA

■ **Dietary diarrhoea**

This can occur as a result of sudden changes in diet, scavenging, feeding unsuitable foods or stress (especially in pups when they go to their new home).

■ **Enteritis**

This is inflammation of the small intestines which can be caused by infection, e.g. parvovirus, a severe worm burden or food poisoning. Continued diarrhoea leads to dehydration.

**Treatment:** treat the original cause, and give a light diet of fish, chicken, scrambled eggs, or a veterinary prescription diet until the stools are normal.

■ **Colitis**

This is inflammation of the large bowel (colon) and symptoms include straining and frequent defecation, watery faeces with mucous or blood, and often an otherwise healthy dog. This is a problem that is frequently encountered in the older Yorkshire Terrier.

**Treatment:** treat the original cause, and give your dog a light diet of fish, chicken, scrambled eggs, or a veterinary prescription diet until the stools are normal. It may be even necessary to change the dog's diet permanently. Ask your vet.

■ **Tumours of the bowel**

These are more likely to cause vomiting than diarrhoea, but one called lymphosarcoma causes diffuse thickening of the gut lining which may lead to diarrhoea.

condition requiring intensive therapy. It can be life-threatening.

■ **Diabetes mellitus**

Another function of the pancreas is to manufacture the hormone insulin, which controls blood sugar levels. If insulin is deficient, blood and urine glucose levels rise, both of which can be detected in laboratory testing. Affected animals have an increased appetite and thirst, weight loss and lethargy. If left untreated, the dog may go into a diabetic coma.

■ **Pancreatic tumours**

These are relatively common and are usually highly malignant. Symptoms vary from vomiting, weight loss and signs of abdominal pain to acute jaundice. The prognosis is usually hopeless, and death rapidly occurs.

## Liver diseases

■ **Acute hepatitis**

Infectious canine hepatitis and leptospirosis (See Infectious Diseases, page 107.) These are not common as most dogs are vaccinated.

■ **Chronic liver failure**

This can be due to heart failure, tumours or cirrhosis. Affected dogs usually lose weight and become depressed, go off their food and may vomit. Diarrhoea and increased thirst are other possible symptoms. The liver may increase or decrease in size, and there is sometimes fluid retention in the abdomen. Jaundice is sometimes apparent. Diagnosis of liver disease depends on symptoms, blood tests, X-rays or ultrasound examination, and possibly liver biopsy.

## SKIN DISEASES

### Itchy skin diseases

#### Parasites

■ **Fleas** are the commonest cause of skin disease, and dogs often become allergic to them. They are dark, fast-moving, sideways-flattened insects, about 2 mm (1/8 in) long.

They spend about two hours a day feeding on the dog, then jump off and spend the rest of the day breeding and laying eggs. They live for about three weeks and can lay twenty eggs a day. Thus each flea may leave behind 400 eggs which hatch out in as little as three weeks. It is important to treat the dog and the environment, e.g. his basket, bedding, surrounding carpet etc. Ask your vet for advice.

### STRUCTURE OF THE SKIN

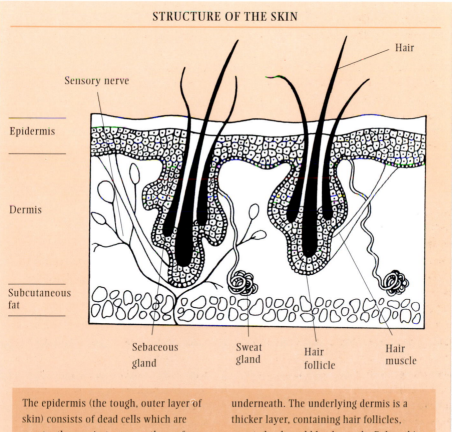

Hair

Sensory nerve

Epidermis

Dermis

Subcutaneous fat

Sebaceous gland

Sweat gland

Hair follicle

Hair muscle

The epidermis (the tough, outer layer of skin) consists of dead cells which are constantly wearing away on the surface and being replaced with new ones from underneath. The underlying dermis is a thicker layer, containing hair follicles, sweat glands and blood vessels. Below this is an insulating layer of subcutaneous fat.

## PARASITES

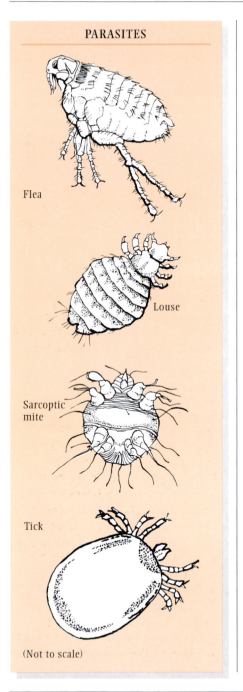

Flea

Louse

Sarcoptic mite

Tick

(Not to scale)

■ **Lice** are small, whitish insects which crawl very slowly between and up the hairs. They lay eggs on the hair, spend their entire life on the dog and are less common and much easier to treat than fleas.

■ **Mange** is caused by a mite (Sarcoptes) which burrows into the skin, causing intense irritation and hair loss. It is very contagious and more common in young dogs. It also spends its entire life on the dog.

■ **Ear mites** cause an itchy ear infection, and appropriate parasiticide drops are needed to correct this condition.

■ **Ticks** (see Non-itchy skin diseases, page 115).

■ **Bacterial infections**

These are common in the dog and are often secondary to some other skin disease, such as mange or allergies.

■ **Pyoderma**

This can be an acute, wet, painful area of the skin (wet eczema), or a more persistent infection appearing as ring-like sores. Both are seen quite commonly in the Yorkshire Terrier.

■ **Furunculosis**

This is a deeper, more serious infection which is seen rarely in the Yorkshire Terrier.

**Treatment:** both bacterial infections require a long course of antibiotics.

■ **Contact dermatitis**

This is an itchy reddening of the skin, usually of the abdomen, groin, armpit or feet, where the hair is thinnest and less protective. It can be an allergic response to materials, such as wool, nylon or carpets, or to a direct irritant, such as oil, or a disinfectant.

■ **Urticaria**

This is seen as the rapid sudden development of itchy lumps in the skin all over the body. It is an allergic response to something that the dog has eaten, breathed in or contacted. It is easily seen as the hairs stand up, but can occur on the face, above the eyes, or in the ears when it is very apparent. The condition is easily reversed by an antihistamine injection, but will sometimes resolve spontaneously.

■ **Lick granuloma**

This is a thickened, hairless patch of skin on the front of the wrist or the side of the ankle, which is seen occasionally in the Yorkshire Terrier. It results from constant licking of this area because of boredom or neurosis.

## Non-itchy skin diseases

■ **Demodectic mange**

Caused by a congenitally-transmitted parasitic mite, this is seen usually in growing dogs, and causes non-itchy patchy hair loss.

■ **Ticks**

These are parasitic spiders resembling small grey peas that attach themselves to the skin. They drop off after a week, but should be removed when noticed. Soak them with surgical spirit and pull them out using fine tweezers.

■ **Ringworm**

This is a fungal infection of the hairs and skin causing bald patches. It is transmissible to man.

■ **Hormonal skin disease**

This patchy, symmetrical hair loss, usually on the flanks, is common in the Yorkshire Terrier. Blood tests are necessary to establish which hormone is involved.

### DISEASES OF THE ANAL AREA

■ **Anal sac impaction**

This is very common. The anal sacs are scent glands and are little used in the dog. If the secretion slowly accumulates in the gland instead of being emptied during defecation, the overful anal sac become itchy. The dog drags

### TUMOURS AND CYSTS

■ **Sebaceous cysts**

These are round, painless nodules in the skin and vary from 2 mm ($^1/_8$ in) up to 4 cm (1 $^1/_2$ in) in diameter.

■ **Warts**

These are quite common in the older dog, and other benign skin tumours do occur.

■ **Anal adenomas**

These frequently develop around the anus in old male dogs. They ulcerate when they are quite small and produce small bleeding points.

his anus along the ground or bites himself around the base of his tail. Unless the sacs are emptied by your vet, an abscess may form.

### DISEASES OF THE FEET

■ **Interdigital eczema**

Dogs readily lick their feet after minor damage, and this makes the feet very wet. Infection then occurs between the pads.

■ **Interdigital cysts and abscesses**

These are painful swellings between the toes which may make the dog lame. In most cases the cause is unknown, but sometimes they can be caused by a grass seed penetrating the skin between the toes, particularly in hairy dogs such as the Yorkie.

■ **Foreign body in the pad**

The most common foreign body is a sharp fragment of glass, or a thorn. The dog is usually very lame and the affected pad painful to the touch. Often an entry point will be seen on the pad.

## STRUCTURE OF THE FOOT

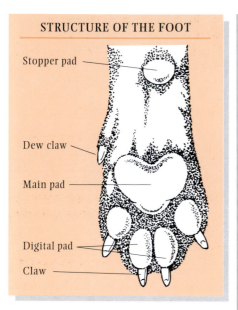

- Stopper pad
- Dew claw
- Main pad
- Digital pad
- Claw

**■ Nail bed infections**

The toe becomes swollen and painful and the dog is lame. The bone may become diseased and this can lead to amputation of the affected toe.

## EAR DISEASES

### Haematoma

A painless, sometimes large blood blister in the ear flap, this is usually caused by head shaking due to an ear infection or irritation.

### Infection (otitis)

Due to his fairly hair-free ear flap, and good ventilation of the ear, the Yorkshire Terrier is not particularly prone to ear infections. When otitis occurs, a smelly discharge appears, and the dog shakes his head or scratches his ear. If the inner ear is affected, the dog may also show a head tilt or a disturbance in his balance.

**Treatment:** antibiotic ear drops are usually successful, but sometimes a surgical operation is needed. The vet must be consulted as there are several possible reasons for ear disease, including ear mites and grass seeds.

### Ear mites

These cause an itchy ear infection, and appropriate parasiticide drops are needed to correct this.

## EYE DISEASES

### Prolapse of the eye

(See First Aid, page 134.)

### Conjunctivitis

This is common in the dog. The white of the eye appears red and discharges. Possible causes include viruses, bacteria, chemicals, allergies, trauma or foreign bodies.

## STRUCTURE OF THE EAR

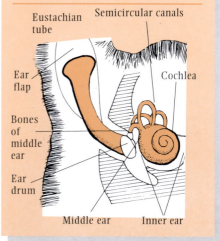

- Eustachian tube
- Semicircular canals
- Ear flap
- Cochlea
- Bones of middle ear
- Ear drum
- Middle ear
- Inner ear

## Keratitis

This is a very sore inflammation of the cornea, which may appear blue and lose its usual shiny appearance.

## Corneal ulcer

This is an erosion of part of the surface of the cornea and can follow an injury or keratitis.

## Cataract

This is an opacity of the lens in one or both eyes. The pupil appears greyish instead of the normal black colour. In advanced cases the lens looks like a pearl and the dog may be blind. The many causes of cataract in Yorkshire Terriers include infection, diabetes mellitus, and trauma.

## URINARY SYSTEM DISEASES

### Diseases producing an increased thirst

■ **Acute kidney failure**

The most common infectious agent producing acute nephritis is Leptospirosis (see Infectious Diseases, page 107).

■ **Chronic kidney failure**

This is common in old dogs and occurs when

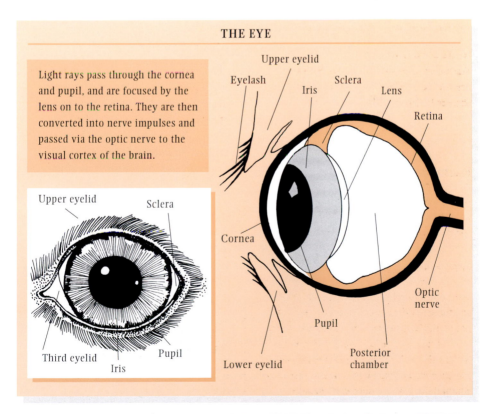

### THE EYE

Light rays pass through the cornea and pupil, and are focused by the lens on to the retina. They are then converted into nerve impulses and passed via the optic nerve to the visual cortex of the brain.

Upper eyelid
Eyelash
Iris
Sclera
Lens
Retina
Cornea
Optic nerve
Pupil
Posterior chamber
Lower eyelid

Upper eyelid
Sclera
Third eyelid
Pupil
Iris

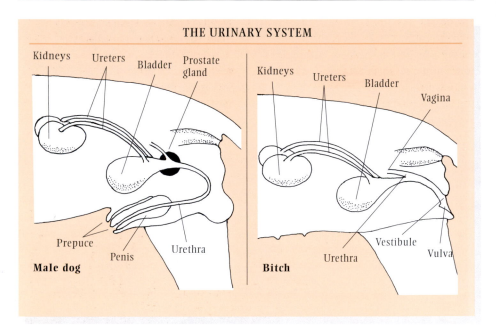

**THE URINARY SYSTEM**

Kidneys  Ureters  Bladder  Prostate gland

Prepuce  Penis  Urethra

**Male dog**

Kidneys  Ureters  Bladder  Vagina

Vestibule  Urethra  Vulva

**Bitch**

persistent damage to the kidney results in toxic substances starting to accumulate in the blood stream.

## Disease causing blood in the urine

■ **Cystitis**
This is an infection of the bladder. It is more common in the bitch because the infection has easy access through the shorter urethra. The clinical signs include:
■ Frequency of urination
■ Straining
■ Sometimes a bloody urine
In all other respects, the dog remains healthy.
■ **Urinary calculi or stones**
These can form in either the kidney or bladder.
■ **Kidney stones** can enter the ureters causing severe abdominal pain.
■ **Bladder stones,** or calculi, are fairly

common in both sexes. In the bitch they are larger and straining is usually the only clinical sign. In the dog the most common sign is unproductive straining due to urinary obstruction.
■ **Tumours of the bladder**
These can occur and cause frequent straining and bloody urine, or by occupying space within the bladder they cause incontinence.
■ **Incontinence**
This occasionally occurs for no apparent reason. Hormones or medicine to tighten the bladder sphincter can help.

## REPRODUCTIVE ORGAN DISEASES

### The male dog

■ **Retained testicle (cryptorchidism)**
Occasionally one or both testicles may fail to

descend into the scrotum and will remain somewhere along their developmental path. Surgery is advisable to remove retained testicles as they are very likely to develop cancer.

■ **Tumours**

These are fairly common but, fortunately, most are benign. One type of testicular tumour,

known as a Sertoli cell tumour, produces female hormones leading to the development of female characteristics.

■ **Prostate disease** is common in the old dog. Usually a benign enlargement occurs where the prostate slowly increases in size. Hormone treatment or castration helps.

## THE REPRODUCTIVE SYSTEM

**The dog**
Sperm and testosterone are produced in the male dog's testicles. Sperm pass into the epididymis for storage and thence via the vas deferens during mating.

**The bitch**
Eggs are produced in the ovaries and enter the uterus through the fallopian tubes. During the heat period, they can be fertilized by sperm.

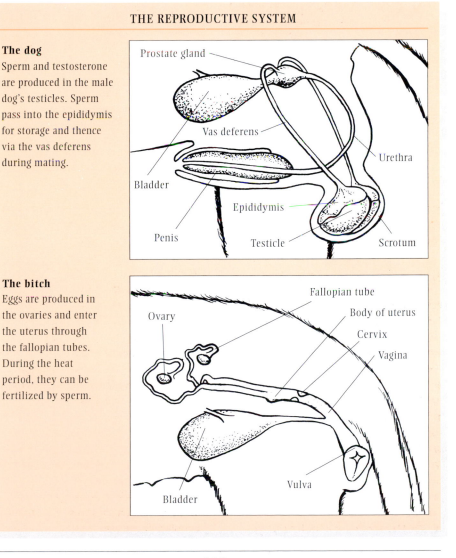

119

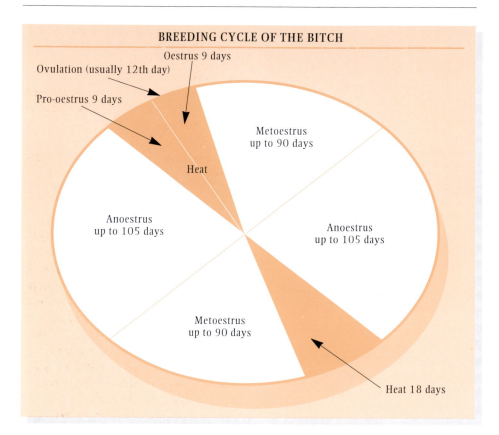

BREEDING CYCLE OF THE BITCH

Oestrus 9 days

Ovulation (usually 12th day)

Pro-oestrus 9 days

Metoestrus
up to 90 days

Heat

Anoestrus
up to 105 days

Anoestrus
up to 105 days

Metoestrus
up to 90 days

Heat 18 days

■ **Infection of the penis and sheath**
(balanitis). An increase and discolouration
occurs in the discharge from the sheath, and the
dog licks his penis more frequently.

■ **Paraphimosis**
This is prolapse of the penis (see First Aid,
page 136).

■ **Castration**
Castration can be of value in the treatment of
certain behavioural problems. Excessive sexual
activity, such as mounting cushions or other
dogs, and territorial urination may be
eliminated by castration, as may certain types
of aggression and the desire for the dog to
escape and wander.

## The bitch

■ **Pyometra**
This is a common and serious disease of the older
bitch although bitches that have had puppies
seem less likely to develop it. The treatment of
choice is usually an ovariohysterectomy.

■ **Mastitis**
This is an infection of the mammary glands and
occurs usually in lactating bitches. The affected
glands become swollen, hard and painful.

■ **Mammary tumours**
These are common in the older entire bitch.
Most are benign, but where malignant, they can
grow rapidly and spread to other organs. Early

## FALSE OR PSEUDO-PREGNANCY

False pregnancy occurs in most bitches about eight to twelve weeks after oestrus at the stage when the bitch would be lactating had she been pregnant. The signs vary and commonly include the following:

- Poor appetite
- Lethargy
- Milk production
- Nest building
- Aggressiveness and attachment to a substitute puppy which is often a squeaky toy

Note that once a bitch has had a false pregnancy, she is likely to have another one after each subsequent heat period.

**Treatment:** if needed, this is by hormones, and prevention is by a hormone injection, or tablets or an ovariohysterectomy.

surgical removal of any lump is advisable because of the danger of malignancy.

## BIRTH CONTROL

- **Hormone therapy**

Several preparations, injections and tablets are available to prevent or postpone the bitch's heat period.

- **Spaying (ovariohysterectomy)**

This is an operation to remove the uterus and ovaries, usually performed when the bitch is not on heat. This is a routine operation and the bitch usually recovers with remarkable speed.

## NERVOUS SYSTEM DISEASES

- **The nervous system**

This consists of two parts:

**1 The central nervous system** (CNS) which consists of the brain and the spinal cord which runs in the vertebral column.

**2 The peripheral nervous system,** including all the nerves that connect the CNS to the organs of the body.

- **Canine distemper virus**

(See Infectious Diseases, page 107.)

- **Vestibular syndrome**

This is a fairly common condition of the older dog, and affects that part of the brain that controls balance. There is a sudden head tilt to the affected side, often flicking movements of the eyes called nystagmus, and the dog may fall or circle to that side. Many dogs will recover slowly but the condition may recur.

- **Slugbait (metaldehyde) poisoning**

The dog appears 'drunk', uncoordinated, and may have convulsions. There is no specific treatment, but sedation will often lead to recovery. Smaller dogs like the Yorkshire Terrier are more at risk as they succumb to a much smaller dose of metaldehyde.

- **Epilepsy**

This is a nervous disorder that is seen occasionally in the Yorkshire Terrier. **Treatment:** this is by the use of anti-convulsant drugs.

## BONE, MUSCLE AND JOINT DISEASES

**Note:** X-rays are necessary to confirm any diagnosis involving bone.

- **Bone infection (osteomyelitis)**

This usually occurs after an injury, such as a bite, or where a broken bone protrudes through the skin. Signs are pain, heat and swelling over the site, and if a limb bone is affected, there can be severe lameness.

■ **Fractures**

Any break or crack in a bone is called a fracture. When a vet repairs a fracture, his aim is to replace the fractured ends of bone into their normal position and then to immobilize the bone for four to six weeks.

Depending on the bone, and type of fracture, there are several methods available, including cage rest, external casts, or surgery to perform internal fixation, by, for example, plating or pinning.

■ **Sprains**

A sprain is an inflammation of an over-stretched joint. The joint is hot, swollen, and painful, and the dog is lame.

## THE SKELETON

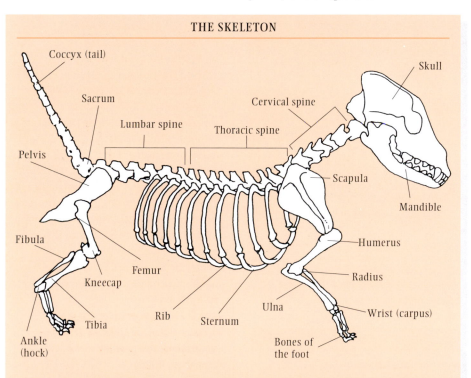

The skeleton is the framework for the body. All the dog's ligaments, muscles and tendons are attached to the bones, 319 of them in total. By a process called ossification, cartilage template is calcified to produce bone. Bones are living tissue and they respond to stresses and strains. To build and keep healthy bones, your Yorkshire Terrier needs a nutritionally balanced diet which contains an adequate supply of calcium, vitamin D and phosphorus.

## TYPES OF FRACTURES

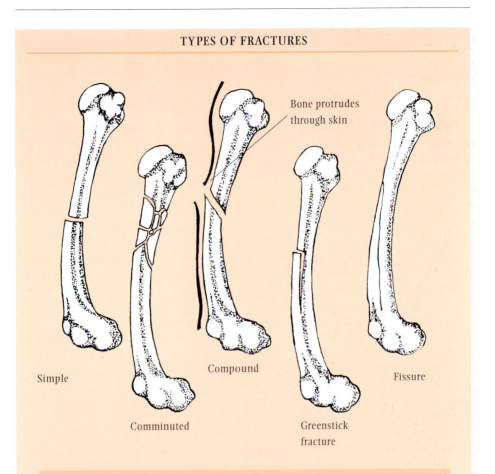

Bone protrudes through skin

Simple

Comminuted

Compound

Greenstick fracture

Fissure

Most broken bones are the result of accidents, especially road traffic ones when dogs are run over by cars. However, puppies are also susceptible to fractures if they are trodden on accidentally or dropped.

If a facture is suspected, you must take the dog to the vet for treatment immediately. Fractures usually heal within six weeks and most dogs regain full mobility.

Five types of fracture are shown above:
- **Simple fracture:** the bone is broken into two pieces at one site
- **Comminuted fracture:** the bone is broken into several pieces
- **Compound fracture:** the skin is penetrated by a broken bone end
- **Greenstick fracture:** the break is incomplete with part of the bone remaining intact
- **Fissure:** the bone is cracked

## PET HEALTH INSURANCE

By choosing your dog wisely in the first place, and then ensuring that he is fit, the right weight, occupied both mentally and physically, protected against disease by vaccination, and fed correctly, you should be able to minimize any vet's bills. The unexpected may well happen though. Accidents and injuries do occur, and dogs can develop lifelong allergies or long-term illnesses such as diabetes. Pet health insurance is available and is recommended by the vast majority of veterinarians for such unexpected eventualities. It is important to take out a policy that will suit you and your Yorkshire Terrier, so it is wise to ask your veterinary surgeon for his recommendation.

■ **Cruciate ligament rupture**

When the cruciate ligament ruptures, as a result of a severe sprain, the stifle or knee joint is destabilized and the dog becomes instantly and severely lame on that leg. This will only usually occur in Yorkshire Terriers if they are middle-aged and overweight. Surgical repair is often necessary.

■ **Arthritis or degenerative joint disease**

This is not common in the Yorkshire Terrier of normal weight. When it occurs, it results in thickening of the joint capsule, formation of abnormal new bone around the edges of the joint and, sometimes, wearing of the joint cartilage. The joint becomes enlarged and painful, and has a reduced range of movement. Arthritis often tends to occur in the older, overweight dog and is usually a problem of the hips, stifles and elbows.

■ **Perthe's Disease**

This is a disease affecting the development of one or both hip joints. It is seen especially in small terriers, and is hereditary in the Yorkshire Terrier. The bone of the head of the femur degenerates, producing severe pain and collapse of the joint (see Special Health Problems of the Yorkshire Terrier, page 105).

■ **Spondylitis**

This is arthritis of the spine. It sometimes occurs in the older Yorkshire Terrier, but it is not common. It causes weakness and stiffness of the hindquarters.

# Chapter nine

# First aid, accidents and emergencies

First aid is the emergency care given to a dog suffering injury or illness of sudden onset.

## Aims of first aid

**1 Keep the dog alive.**
**2 Prevent unnecessary suffering.**
**3 Prevent further injury.**

## Rules of first aid

### 1

**Keep calm.** If you panic you will be unable to help effectively.

### 2

**Contact a vet as soon as possible.** Advice given over the telephone may be life-saving.

### 3

**Avoid injury to yourself.** A distressed or injured animal may bite so use a muzzle if necessary (see muzzling, page 136).

### 4

**Control haemorrhage.** Excessive blood loss can lead to severe shock and death (see haemorrhage, page 129).

### 5

**Maintain an airway**. Failure to breathe or obtain adequate oxygen can lead to brain damage or loss of life within five minutes (see airway obstruction and artificial respiration, page 127).

## Common accidents and emergencies

The following common accidents and emergencies all require first aid action. In an emergency, your priorities are to keep the dog alive and comfortable until he can be examined by a vet. In many cases, there is effective action that you can take immediately to help preserve your dog's health and life.

# SHOCK AND ROAD ACCIDENTS

## SHOCK

This is a serious clinical syndrome which can cause death. Shock can follow road accidents, severe burns, electrocution, extremes of heat and cold, heart failure, poisoning, severe fluid loss, reactions to drugs, insect stings or snake bite.

**SIGNS OF SHOCK**
- Weakness or collapse
- Pale gums
- Cold extremities, e.g. feet and ears
- Weak pulse and rapid heart
- Rapid, shallow breathing

### RECOMMENDED ACTION

**1** Act immediately. Give cardiac massage (see page 128) and/or artificial respiration (see page 127) if necessary, after checking for a clear airway.

**2** Keep the dog flat and warm. Control external haemorrhage (page 129).

**3** Veterinary treatment is essential thereafter.

## ROAD ACCIDENTS

Injuries resulting from a fast-moving vehicle colliding with an animal can be very serious. Road accidents may result in:
- Death
- Head injuries
- Spinal damage
- Internal haemorrhage, bruising and rupture of major organs, e.g. liver, spleen, kidneys
- Fractured ribs and lung damage, possibly resulting in haemothorax (blood in the chest cavity) or pneumothorax (air in the chest cavity)
- Fractured limbs with or without nerve damage
- External haemorrhage, wounds, tears and bruising

### RECOMMENDED ACTION

**1** Assess the situation and move the dog to a safe position. Use a blanket to transport him and keep him flat.

**2** Check for signs of life: feel for a heart beat (see cardiac massage, page 128), and watch for the rise and fall of the chest wall to indicate breathing.

**3** If the dog is breathing, treat as for shock (see above). If he is not breathing but there is a heart beat, give artificial respiration, after checking for airway obstruction. Consider the use of a muzzle (see muzzling, page 136).

**4** Control external haemorrhage (see haemorrhage, page 129).

**5** Keep the dog warm and flat at all times, and seek veterinary help.

## AIRWAY OBSTRUCTION

■ **FOREIGN BODY IN THE THROAT,** e.g. a ball or marble.

### RECOMMENDED ACTION

**1**

This is an acute emergency. Do not try to pull out the object. Push it upwards and forwards from behind the throat so that it moves from its position in the throat, where it is obstructing the larynx, into the mouth.

**2**

The dog should now be able to breathe. Remove the object from his mouth.

■ **TRACHEAL COLLAPSE** (see Special Health Problems, page 105.)

## DROWNING

### RECOMMENDED ACTION

**1** When out of the water, remove the collar and place the dog on his side with his head lower than his body.

**2** With your hands, apply firm downward pressure at five-second intervals on the chest.

■ **FOLLOWING A ROAD ACCIDENT**, or convulsion, blood, saliva or vomit in the throat may obstruct breathing.

### RECOMMENDED ACTION

**1**

Pull the tongue forwards and clear any obstruction with your fingers.

**2**

Then, with the dog on his side, extend the head and neck forwards to maintain a clear airway.

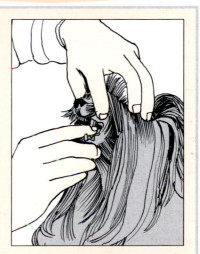

## ARTIFICIAL RESPIRATION

This is the method for helping a dog which has a clear airway but cannot breathe.

### RECOMMENDED ACTION

Use mouth-to-mouth resuscitation by cupping your hands over his nose and mouth and blowing into his nostrils every five seconds.

# CARDIAC MASSAGE

This is required if your dog's heart fails.

## RECOMMENDED ACTION

### 1

With the dog lying on his right side, feel for a heart beat with your fingers on the chest wall behind the dog's elbows on his left side.

### 2

If you feel nothing, squeeze rhythmically with your palms, placing one hand on top of the other, as shown, at two-second intervals, pressing down hard.

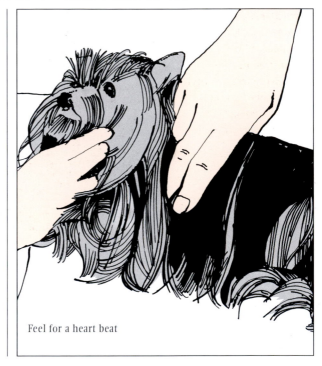

Feel for a heart beat

Applying cardiac massage

# HAEMORRHAGE

Severe haemorrhage must be controlled, as it leads to a precipitous fall in blood pressure and the onset of shock. Haemorrhage is likely to result from deep surface wounds, or internal injuries, e.g. following a road accident.

■ **FOR SURFACE WOUNDS**

> RECOMMENDED
> ACTION

Locate the bleeding point and apply pressure either with:
- **Your thumb** or
- **A pressure bandage** (preferred method) or
- **A tourniquet**

**1** **Pressure bandage**
Use a pad of gauze, cotton wool or cloth against the wound and tightly bandage around it. In the

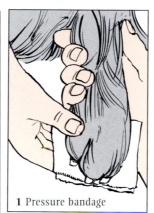

1 Pressure bandage

absence of a proper dressing, use a clean handkerchief or scarf.

**2** If the bleeding continues, apply another dressing on top of the first.

**1** **Tourniquet** (on limbs and tail)
Tie a narrow piece of cloth, a neck tie or dog lead tightly

Tourniquet

around the limb, nearer to the body than the wound itself.

**2** Using a pencil or stick within the knot, twist until it becomes tight enough to stop the blood flow.

**3** **Important**: you must seek veterinary assistance as soon as possible.

**Note:** Tourniquets should be applied for no longer than fifteen minutes at a time, or tissue death may result.

■ **FOR INTERNAL BLEEDING**

> RECOMMENDED
> ACTION

**1** You should keep the animal quiet and warm, and minimize any movement.

**2** **Important**: you must seek veterinary assistance as soon as possible.

2 Pressure bandage

# WOUNDS

These may result from road accidents, dog fights, sharp stones or glass, etc. Deep wounds may cause serious bleeding, bone or nerve damage.

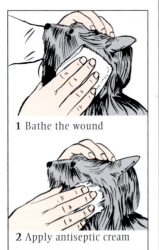

1 Bathe the wound

2 Apply antiseptic cream

## RECOMMENDED ACTION

**1** Deal with external bleeding (see haemorrhage, page 129) and keep the dog quiet before seeking veterinary attention.

**2** Cut feet or pads should be bandaged to prevent further blood loss.

**3** Minor cuts, abrasions and bruising should be bathed with warm salt solution (one 5ml teaspoonful per 550ml (1 pint) of water). They should be protected from further injury or contamination. Apply some antiseptic cream, if necessary.

**4** If in doubt, ask your vet to check in case the wound needs suturing or antibiotic therapy, particularly if caused by fighting. Even minor cuts and punctures can be complicated by the presence of a foreign body.

# FRACTURES

Broken bones often result from road accidents, especially in the legs. Be careful when lifting and transporting the affected dog.

■ **LEG FRACTURES**

## RECOMMENDED ACTION

**1** Broken lower leg bones can sometimes be straightened gently, bandaged and then taped or tied with string to a make-shift splint, e.g. a piece of wood or rolled-up newspaper or cardboard.

**2** Otherwise, support the leg to prevent any movement. Take the dog to the vet immediately.

■ **OTHER FRACTURES**
These may be more difficult to diagnose. If you suspect a fracture, transport your dog very gently with great care, and get him to the vet.

# OTHER ACCIDENTS AND EMERGENCIES

## COLLAPSE

This may be accompanied by loss of consciousness, but not in every case.

**POSSIBLE CAUSES**

- Head trauma, e.g. following a road accident
- Heart failure
- Stroke
- Hyperthermia (heat-stroke)
- Hypothermia (cold)
- Hypocalcaemia (low calcium)
- Shock
- Spinal fractures
- Asphyxia (interference with breathing)
- Electrocution
- Poisoning
- Tracheal collapse

**Note:** you should refer to the relevant section for further details of these problems.

### RECOMMENDED ACTION

**1** The collapsed animal must be moved with care to avoid further damage.

**2** Gently slide him on his side onto a coat or a blanket.

**3** Check he is breathing, and then keep him quiet and warm until you obtain professional help.

**4** If he is not breathing, administer artificial respiration immediately, after checking for a clear airway (see page 127).

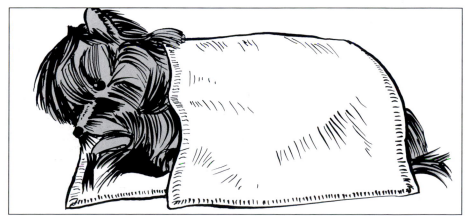

Other accidents and emergencies

## CONVULSIONS (FITS OR SEIZURES)

These are very alarming to dog owners. Uncontrolled spasms, 'paddling' of legs, loss of consciousness, sometimes salivation and involuntary urination or defecation occur. Most convulsions only last a few minutes, but the dog is often confused and dazed afterwards.

**POSSIBLE CAUSES**

- Poisoning
- Head injuries
- Brain tumours
- Liver and kidney disease
- Meningitis
- Epilepsy
- Low blood glucose, e.g. in diabetes, or low blood calcium, e.g. in eclampsia

### RECOMMENDED ACTION

**1** Unless he is in a dangerous situation, do not attempt to hold the dog, but protect him from damaging himself.

 **2** Do not give him anything by mouth.

**3** Try to keep him quiet, cool and in a darkened room until he sees the vet.

**4** If you have to move him, cover him with a blanket first.

## HEART FAILURE

This is not as common in dogs as in humans. Affected dogs faint, usually during exercise, and lose consciousness. The mucous membranes appear pale or slightly blue.

### RECOMMENDED ACTION

**1** Cover the dog in a blanket, and lie him on his side.

**2** Massage his chest behind the elbows (see cardiac massage, page 128).

**3** When he recovers, take him straight to the vet.

**1** An affected dog should be covered with a blanket and laid on his side.
**2** Apply cardiac massage, pressing down firmly at two-second intervals.

## HEAT-STROKE

This occurs in hot weather, especially when dogs have been left in cars with insufficient ventilation. Affected animals are extremely distressed, panting and possibly collapsed. They can die rapidly. A heat-stroke case should be treated as an acute emergency.

### RECOMMENDED ACTION

**1** Place the dog in a cold bath or run cold water over his body until his temperature is in the normal range.

**2** Offer water with added salt (one 5ml teaspoonful per half litre (18 fl oz) water).

**3** Treatment for shock may be necessary (see page 126).

## ELECTROCUTION

This is most likely to occur in a bored puppy who chews through a cable. Electrocution may kill him outright or lead to delayed shock.

■ **DO NOT TOUCH HIM BEFORE YOU SWITCH OFF THE ELECTRICITY SOURCE.**

### RECOMMENDED ACTION

**1** If he is not breathing, begin artificial respiration immediately (see page 127) and keep him warm.

**2** Contact your vet; if he survives he will need treatment for shock (see page 126).

## BURNS AND SCALDS

**POSSIBLE CAUSES**
■ Spilled hot drinks, boiling water or fat
■ Friction, chemical and electrical burns

### RECOMMENDED ACTION

**1** Immediately apply running cold water and, thereafter, cold compresses, ice packs or packets of frozen peas to the affected area.

**2** Veterinary attention is essential in most cases.

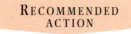

## SNAKE BITE

This is due to the adder in Great Britain. Signs are pain accompanied by a soft swelling around two puncture wounds, usually on either the head, neck or limbs. Trembling, collapse, shock and even death can ensue.

### RECOMMENDED ACTION

**1** Do not let the dog walk; carry him to the car.

**2** Keep him warm, and take him immediately to the vet.

# FOREIGN BODIES

- **IN THE MOUTH**

Sticks or bones wedged between the teeth cause frantic pawing at the mouth and salivation.

### RECOMMENDED ACTION

Remove the foreign body with your fingers or pliers, using a wooden block placed between the dog's canine teeth if possible to aid the safety of this procedure. Some objects have to be removed under general anaesthesia.

**Note:** a ball in the throat is dealt with in airway obstruction (see page 127), and is a critical emergency.

- **FISH HOOKS**

Never try to pull these out, wherever they are.

### RECOMMENDED ACTION

Push the fish hook through the skin, cut the end with pliers and then push the barbed end through.

- **IN THE EAR – GRASS SEEDS**

These are the little spiky seeds of the wild barley, and are a real nuisance to dogs. If one finds its way into an ear, it can produce sudden severe distress and violent head shaking.

### RECOMMENDED ACTION

If you can see the seed, gently but firmly pull it out with tweezers, and check it is intact. If you cannot see it, or feel you may have left some in, call the vet immediately.

- **IN THE FOOT**

Glass, thorns or splinters can penetrate the pads or soft skin, causing pain, and infection if neglected.

### RECOMMENDED ACTION

Soak the foot in warm salt water and then use a sharp sterilized needle or pair of tweezers to extract the foreign body. If this is not possible, take your dog to the vet who will remove it under local or general anaesthetic if necessary.

# NOSE BLEEDS

These may be caused by trauma or violent sneezing, but are also related in some cases to ulceration of the lining of the nasal cavity.

### RECOMMENDED ACTION

**1** Keep the dog quiet and use ice packs on the bridge of the nose.

**2** Contact your vet if the bleeding persists.

# EYEBALL PROLAPSE

Not a common problem in the Yorkshire Terrier, but it may arise from head trauma, e.g. following a dog fight. The eye is forced out of its socket and sight is lost unless it is replaced within fifteen minutes.

### RECOMMENDED ACTION

**1** Speed is essential. One person should pull the eyelids apart while the other gently presses the eyeball back into its socket, using moist sterile gauze or cloth.

**2** If this is impossible, cover the eye with moist sterile gauze and take him to your vet immediately.

# GASTRIC DILATION

This is an emergency and cannot be treated at home. The stomach distends with gas and froth which the dog cannot easily eliminate. In some cases, the stomach then rotates and a torsion occurs, so the gases cannot escape at all and the stomach rapidly fills the abdomen. This causes pain, respiratory distress and circulatory failure. Life-threatening shock follows.

### PREVENTIVE ACTION

**1** Avoid the problem by not exercising your dog vigorously for two hours after a full meal.

**2** If your dog is becoming bloated and has difficulty breathing, he is unlikely to survive unless he has veterinary attention within half an hour of the onset of symptoms, so get him to the vet immediately.

# POISONING

Dogs can be poisoned by pesticides, herbicides, poisonous plants, paints, antifreeze or an overdose of drugs (animal or human).

■ If poisoning is suspected, first try to determine the agent involved, and find out if it is corrosive or not. This may be indicated on the container, but may also be evident from the blistering of the lips, gums and tongue, and increased salivation.

### RECOMMENDED ACTION

■ **CORROSIVE POISONS**

**1** Wash the inside of the dog's mouth.

**2** Give him milk and bread to protect the gut against the effects of the corrosive.

**3** Seek veterinary help.

■ **OTHER POISONS**

**1** If the dog is conscious, make him vomit within half an hour of taking the poison.

**2** A crystal of washing soda or a few 15ml tablespoonfuls of strong salt solution can be given carefully by mouth.

**3** Retain a sample of vomit to aid identification of the poison, or take the poison container with you to show the vet. There may be an antidote, and any information can help in treatment.

# STINGS

Bee and wasp stings often occur around the head, front limbs or mouth. The dog usually shows sudden pain and paws at, or licks, the stung area. A soft, painful swelling appears; sometimes the dog seems unwell or lethargic. Stings in the mouth and throat can be distressing and dangerous.

### RECOMMENDED ACTION

**1** Withdraw the sting (bees).

**2** Then you can bathe the area in:
■ Vinegar for wasps
■ Bicarbonate for bees

**3** An antihistamine injection may be needed.

OTHER ACCIDENTS AND EMERGENCIES

# BREEDING

## ECLAMPSIA

This is an emergency which may occur when your Yorkie bitch is suckling puppies, usually when the pups are about three weeks old. It is a very serious condition and can be fatal. The blood calcium level of the bitch becomes low due to the pups' demands on her milk, and she starts to show nervous symptoms. Initially she starts to twitch or shiver and appears unsteady. This rapidly progresses to staggering, then convulsions. There is no first aid except administering calcium tablets or liquid. Keep her warm and consult your vet immediately.

## PARAPHIMOSIS

*(See page 120)*
This problem may occur after mating, in the male Yorkie. It is caused by a prolonged erection of the penis which is unable to retract back into the sheath after mating. It becomes very swollen due to constriction by the sheath. The exposed penis should be bathed in cool sterile water to reduce it in size, and lubrication with petroleum jelly or soap should make it possible to pull the sheath forward over the penis. If correction proves impossible, veterinary help is needed.

# MUZZLING

This will allow a nervous, distressed or injured dog to be examined safely, without the risk of being bitten. A tape or bandage is secured around the muzzle as illustrated. However, a muzzle should not be applied in the following circumstances:

■ Airway obstruction
■ Loss of consciousness
■ Compromised breathing or severe chest injury

1 Tie a knot in the bandage.
2 Wrap around the dog's muzzle with the knot under the lower jaw.
3 Tie firmly behind the dog's head.

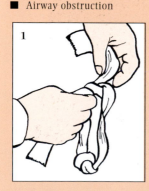

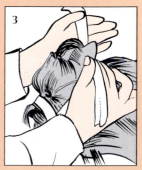

**Angulation**
The angles created by bones meeting at a joint.

**Breed standard**
The description laid down by the Kennel Club of the perfect breed specimen.

**Brood bitch**
A female dog which is used for breeding.

**Carpals**
These are the wrist bones.

**Croup**
This is the dog's rump: the front of the pelvis to the start of the tail.

**Dam**
The mother of puppies.

**Dew claw**
A fifth toe above the ground on the inside of the legs.

**Elbow**
The joint at the top of the forearm below the upper arm.

**Flank**
The area between the last rib and hip on the side of the body.

**Furnishings**
The long hair on the head, legs, thighs, back of buttocks or tail.

**Gait**
How a dog moves at different speeds.

**Guard hairs**
Long hairs that grow through the undercoat.

**Muzzle**
The foreface, or front of the head.

**Occiput**
The back upper part of the skull.

**Oestrus**
The periods when a bitch is 'on heat' or 'in season' and responsive to mating.

**Pastern**
Between the wrist (carpus) and the digits of the forelegs.

**Scissor bite**
Strong jaws with upper teeth overlapping lower ones.

**Stifle**
The hind leg joint, or 'knee'.

**Undercoat**
A dense, short coat hidden below the top-coat.

**Whelping**
The act of giving birth.

**Whelps**
Puppies that have not been weaned.

**Whiskers**
Long hairs on the jaw and muzzle.

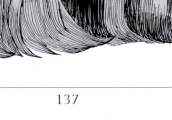

# INDEX

## FURTHER READING (PERIODICALS)

**Dogs Monthly**
R T C Associates, Ascot House
High Street, Ascot
Berks SL5 7JG

**Dogs Today**
Pet Subjects Ltd
Pankhurst Farm, Bagshot Road

West End, Nr Woking
Surrey GU24 9QR

**Dog Training Weekly**
4/5 Feidr Castell Business
Park,
Fishguard
Dyfed SA65 9BB

**Dog World**
9 Tufton Street
Ashford, Kent TN23 1QN

**Our Dogs**
5 Oxford Road,
Station Approach
Manchester M60 1SX

# USEFUL ADDRESSES

**Animal Aunts**
Smugglers
Green Lane
Rogate
Petersfield
Hampshire
GU31 5DA
(Home sitters, holidays)

**Association of Pet**
**Behaviour Counsellors**
PO Box 46
Worcester
WR8 9YS

**British Veterinary**
**Association**
7 Mansfield Street
London
W1G 9NQ

**Dog Breeders Insurance**
**Co Ltd**
9 St Stephens Court
St Stephens Road
Bournemouth
BH2 6LG
(Books of cover notes for
dog breeders)

**Featherbed**
**Country Club**
High Wycombe
Bucks
HP15 6XP
(Luxury dog accommodation)

**Guide Dogs for the**
**Blind Association**
Burghfield Common
Reading
RG7 3YG

**Hearing Dogs for the Deaf**
The Training Centre
London Road
Lewknor
Oxon OX9 5RY

**The Kennel Club**
1-5 Clarges Street
Piccadilly
London W1Y 8AB
(Breed Standards, Breed Club
and Field Trial contact
addresses, registration forms,
Good Citizen training scheme)

**National Canine**
**Defence League**
17 Wakeley Street
London
EC1V 7RQ

**Pets As Therapy**
**(PAT Dogs)**
10a Welldon Cres
Harrow
Middlesex
HA1 1QT
(Information: how friendly
dogs can join the hospital
visiting scheme)

**PRO Dogs**
**National Charity**
4 New Road
Ditton
Kent
ME20 6AD
(Information: Better British
Breeders, worming certificates
to provide with puppies, how
to cope with grief on the loss
of a loved dog etc.)

**Royal Society for the**
**Prevention of Cruelty**
**to Animals**
RSPCA Headquarters
Wilberforce Way
Southwater
Horsham
West Sussex
RH12 1HG

**WitsEnd School**
**for Dogs**
Scampers Petcare Superstore
Northfield Crossroads
Soham
Ely
Cambs CB7 5UF
Tel: 01353 727111

CANCELLED